MARGINALIA TO STONE BIRD

Conversation Pieces

A Small Paperback Series from Aqueduct Press
Subscriptions available: www.aqueductpress.com

1. The Grand Conversation
   Essays by L. Timmel Duchamp
2. With Her Body
   Short Fiction by Nicola Griffith
3. Changeling
   A Novella by Nancy Jane Moore
4. Counting on Wildflowers
   An Entanglement by Kim Antieau
5. The Traveling Tide
   Short Fiction by Rosaleen Love
6. The Adventures of the Faithful Counselor
   A Narrative Poem by Anne Sheldon
7. Ordinary People
   A Collection by Eleanor Arnason
8. Writing the Other
   A Practical Approach
   by Nisi Shawl & Cynthia Ward
9. Alien Bootlegger
   A Novella by Rebecca Ore
10. The Red Rose Rages (Bleeding)
    A Short Novel by L. Timmel Duchamp
11. Talking Back: Epistolary Fantasies
    edited by L. Timmel Duchamp
12. Absolute Uncertainty
    Short Fiction by Lucy Sussex
13. Candle in a Bottle
    A Novella by Carolyn Ives Gilman

14. Knots
    Short Fiction by Wendy Walker

15. Naomi Mitchison: A Profile of Her Life and Work
    A Monograph by Lesley A. Hall

16. We, Robots
    A Novella by Sue Lange

17. Making Love in Madrid
    A Novella by Kimberly Todd Wade

18. Of Love and Other Monsters
    A Novella by Vandana Singh

19. Aliens of the Heart
    Short Fiction by Carolyn Ives Gilman

20. Voices From Fairyland:
    The Fantastical Poems of Mary Coleridge, Charlotte Mew, and Sylvia Townsend Warner
    Edited and With Poems by Theodora Goss

21. My Death
    A Novella by Lisa Tuttle

22. De Secretis Mulierum
    A Novella by L. Timmel Duchamp

23. Distances
    A Novella by Vandana Singh

24. Three Observations and a Dialogue:
    Round and About SF
    Essays by Sylvia Kelso and a correspondence with Lois McMaster Bujold

25. The Buonarotti Quartet
    Short Fiction by Gwyneth Jones

26. Slightly Behind and to the Left
    Four Stories & Three Drabbles by Claire Light

27. Through the Drowsy Dark
    Short Fiction and Poetry by Rachel Swirsky

28. Shotgun Lullabies
    Stories and Poems by Sheree Renée Thomas

29. A Brood of Foxes
    A Novella by Kristin Livdahl

30. The Bone Spindle
    Poems and Short Fiction by Anne Sheldon

31. The Last Letter
    A Novella by Fiona Lehn

32. We Wuz Pushed
    On Joanna Russ and Radical Truth-Telling
    by Brit Mandelo

33. The Receptionist and Other Tales
    Poems by Lesley Wheeler

34. Birds and Birthdays
    Stories by Christopher Barzak

35. The Queen, the Cambion, and Seven Others
    Stories by Richard Bowes

36. Spring in Geneva
    A Novella by Sylvia Kelso

37. The XY Conspiracy
    A Novella by Lori Selke

38. Numa
    An Epic Poem
    by Katrinka Moore

39. Myths, Metaphors, and Science Fiction:
    Ancient Roots of the Literature of the Future
    Essays by Sheila Finch

40. NoFood
    Short Fiction by Sarah Tolmie

41. The Haunted Girl
    Poems and Short Stories by Lisa M. Bradley

42. Three Songs for Roxy
    A Novella by Caren Gussoff

43. Ghost Signs
    Poems and a Short Story by Sonya Taaffe

44. The Prince of the Aquamarines & The Invisible
    Prince: Two Fairy Tales
    by Louise Cavelier Levesque

45. Back, Belly, and Side: True Lies and False Tales
    by Celeste Rita Baker

46. A Day in Deep Freeze
    A Novella by Lisa Shapter

47. A Field Guide to the Spirits
    Poems by Jean LeBlanc

48. Marginalia to Stone Bird
    Poems by Rose Lemberg

About the Aqueduct Press Conversation Pieces Series

The feminist engaged with sf is passionately interested in challenging the way things are, passionately determined to understand how everything works. It is my constant sense of our feminist-sf present as a grand conversation that enables me to trace its existence into the past and from there see its trajectory extending into our future. A genealogy for feminist sf would not constitute a chart depicting direct lineages but would offer us an ever-shifting, fluid mosaic, the individual tiles of which we will probably only ever partially access. What could be more in the spirit of feminist sf than to conceptualize a genealogy that explicitly manifests our own communities across not only space but also time?

Aqueduct's small paperback series, Conversation Pieces, aims to both document and facilitate the "grand conversation." The Conversation Pieces series presents a wide variety of texts, including short fiction (which may not always be sf and may not necessarily even be feminist), essays, speeches, manifestoes, poetry, interviews, correspondence, and group discussions. Many of the texts are reprinted material, but some are new. The grand conversation reaches at least as far back as Mary Shelley and extends, in our speculations and visions, into the continually-created future. In Jonathan Goldberg's words, "To look forward to the history that will be, one must look at and retell the history that has been told." And that is what Conversation Pieces is all about.

L. Timmel Duchamp

Jonathan Goldberg, "The History That Will Be" in Louise Fradenburg and Carla Freccero, eds., *Premodern Sexualities* (New York and London: Routledge, 1996)

Published by Aqueduct Press
PO Box 95787
Seattle, WA 98145-2787
www.aqueductpress.com

 First Edition, January 2016

10 9 8 7 6 5 4 3 2 1

ISBN: 978-1-61976-099-8

See Acknowledgments for previous publications.

Cover photograph courtesy Aleksei Kruhlenia

The Market Square in Bruges, Belgium.

Original Block Print of Mary Shelley by Justin Kempton:
www.writersmugs.com

Printed in the USA by Applied Digital Imaging

Conversation Pieces

Volume 48

MARGINALIA TO STONE BIRD

by

Rose Lemberg

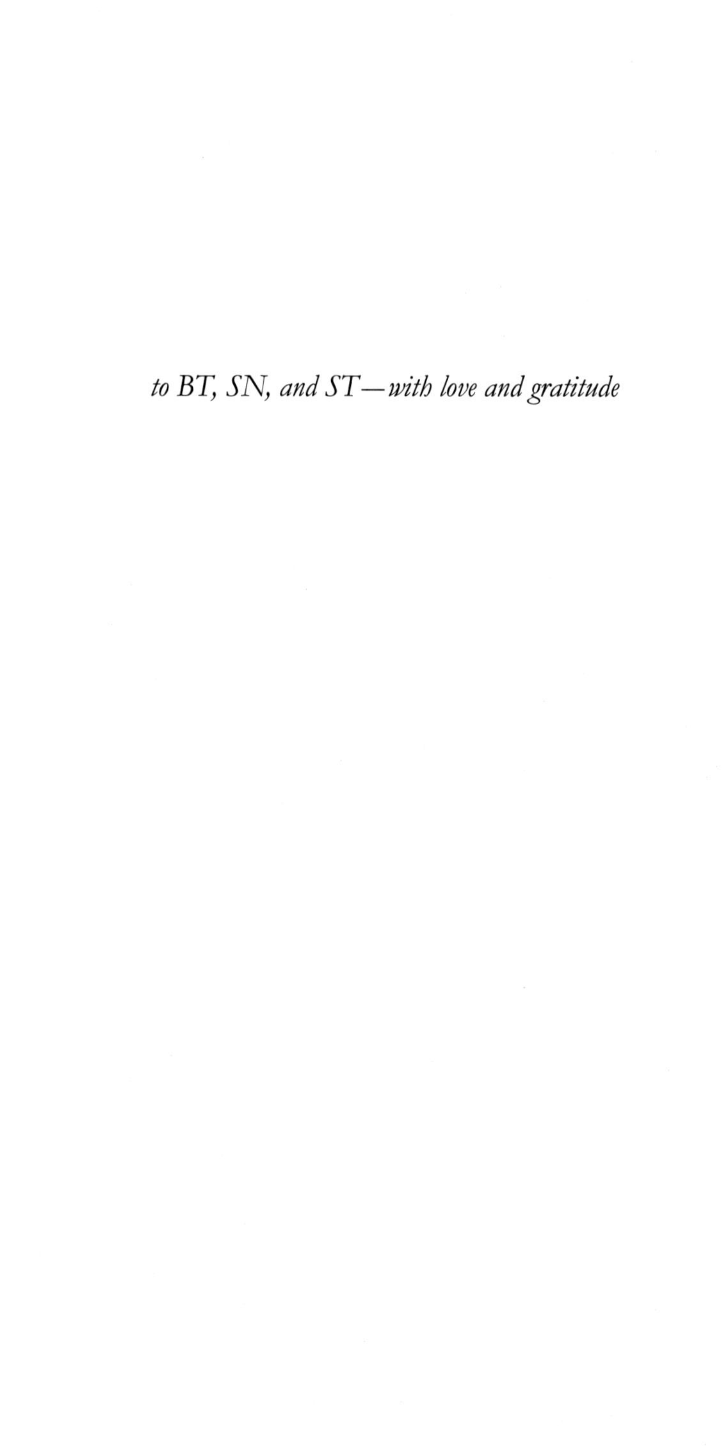

to BT, SN, and ST—with love and gratitude

Contents

Burns at Both Ends

If you burn this fierce, firebird,
you'll finish yourself off,
you'll die young, they said.
I tried slow, sluggishly,
ended up beige and feeling like gruel.
Who cares about tepid? Better the sizzling
feathers of nightmares,
the flesh of desire subjected to torturous time.
Old age doesn't scare me. I'll live as haphazardly as before,
dropping clutter and rubies wherever I walk.

Finding Voice

The Three Immigrations

First immigration–The Strangers of the Glass

in dress of handblown cinnamon and blue
and speaking speckled bubbles in the glass;
Their power is to come and pour a road—
to molt the land for us,
then leave

[The In-between]

with luggage of caramel leather and brass locks—no,
there's no romance in this travel. Only a crumbled
book in Yiddish and a tin
of buttons *(remember the horn one from grandmother's*
mustard dress she wore on the train to…) cut from all the old
dresses, and grandmother's
death certificate is ten days old. A plastic bag
of photographs. A dry salami.
In Hungary, they put us behind bars.

A Mini-Map

There are two waters in my land
bridged by a road of molten glass,
and if you step on it, you'll pass
outside of tenses:
neither past, nor present, nor a future, nor
(first, second, third) a person (singular or plural)
instead, a being on the road of glass

[In Hungary, they put us behind bars]

to wait for the plane. Like rats in a ca- /
people / sheep to the sla- / *(now you cross out)*
My grandmother's ghost
struggled to follow us, but lost her way
somewhere in the fields between point A
and the warehouse. They didn't
let us peek out. My father said
Budapest must be beautiful

Second Immigration –
The Strangers in Soldiers' Clothing

war-tossed in weeping ships
they arrive at Northwater. They left behind
everything,
even the ocean. Brought only the bell
forged by citymakers
by true voice-makers in the old country. The song
tolls the dead into their new earth. They build
a church at Graveyard Island, and hang
their voice there; then on
to the road of glass

[Arriving, the Gulf War]

is the first thing I remember. Bombs falling, and a gaping
hole in the wall. Sirens. A family of four,
we locked ourselves in the bathroom. The gas mask smelled
like gas, or burnt rubber,
or a language.
Cockroaches ate
my mother's salvaged wedding dress, and I learned
to speak; made up three languages to hide in

Beginnings are endings

When they reached Southwater, the war clothing
seeped into their skins and they as speechless as fish
that clog the glassroad,
fish for the souls of the dead
scraped onto the glass.
They settled by the Southwater,
walled off a city there. Called her Bell,
or perhaps—
  nothing.

Third Immigration–The Strangers with Animals

They come joyfully, bringing only
their most beloved ones—a small city
guarded by white beasts in the heart of one person; another
carries a snake abjad to spell the truth
in blunt consonants. Another's heart
protects the bird of vowels.
Shall they unlock
the larynx of love and longing, or shall they step
onto the road of molten glass?

[I was so terrified, I don't remember]

a thing of that last journey. I'd packed
two changes of clothing (my mother had bought me
four-inch heels with her last money; I cannot
wear them, but have no other shoes).
Three books—
a battered copy
of the Poetic Edda in Old Norse, Biblia
Hebraica Stuttgartensia, and Ted Hughes' *Crow*.
I do not remember
how they stood—my father speaking
for the last time, or my mother—

before his stroke. I do not remember
how the plane smelled, or the long winding line
at immigration services.
Alone.
In the future of me, the San Francisco Bay Bridge
circles my head like a red dragon crown.

Coda: I made three languages

to hide in. Each within
the only land I've ever called my own
between the waters. I am still the same
or am I? How to know
if all my journeys are translated in the skin
or am I dithering
before the road of glass?

Resh

I have scratched off these cave-walls
the abjad in which the self is transcribed,
that script without vowels, desert-parched, unaware
of oceans—but a sheen of sweat
rises from the walls like dew,
three thousand years after the miners.

I don't need to return here,
where I've toiled these lives and years ago,
a turquoise miner who paid the stone back in tears,
who carved crooked symbols when nobody watched.
I have been here, I have passed,
with only myself to erase me
bending down from future immemorial.

Circumscribed by sweat and turquoise dust, hidden
in folds of the star-embroidered night,
I dreamed myself into this future, not knowing
of perils—of sorrows that constrict me
tighter than collars of blistering stone. I did not think
that I would forget me, and yet grieve
for languages that have been lost between us,
three thousand years of mothers' names gone.

I have erased and reinscribed
both of us onto the stone page of my story.
Easy to say that nothing's been lost,
but I don't know what I am overwriting
when none is here to slap my wrist.

How can I speak for us even if you're me,
type what it felt to wake in that cave-mine hungry,
to scratch wordselves into the indifferent rock?

But our abjads are almost the same;
I carve resh for my name,
for memory's not the extent of it, not
when the dry desert wind still blows between us.

Odysseus on the war train

My hero, when you left Penelope did you
imagine never stepping off this train? Its every wagon
a Trojan horse that carries soldiers far from home
and every Trojan horse a coffin. You would seek
adventure, but your paramours are rotting
like empty grain-stalks in deserted fields and skulls
of babies smashed against the walls and husbands rotting
in battlefields—you too were eager to depart.
She will remake, you say, the tapestry and bring you home
and wash your feet and make your bed again—but she unravels
your roads each night. Unmakes the language, spreads
the shroud of silence over you, and prays you never
return.

Dybbuk Song

When I hung between heaven and non-existence, tormented by spirits that sputtered white and slender between the worlds gone black, I saw your soul burning to me from beyond the curtain that separates the living from us, that letter by letter presses us out into the void; and I sang, to you, and you to me.

Will you call me an affliction? Me, a sticking spirit that has wheedled back into this world through tiny holes left by letters embroidered upon the veil that separates the living from unliving—me, who squeezed through holes embroidery needles left in the tapestry of the letters of your life—me, who acquired a lettershape to reach you

Which letter will you choose for me, which letter shall you sing—a consonant, a mem, a shape of water—carry it in your palm and spill it, carry it close to your mouth and ask me: why are you here?

To atone for sins, I whisper, an always-answer, an expected answer—to atone for that which I don't hold as sinful; for you, through you, I will fulfill the 613 commandments I have neglected in my life; I will weave tsitsit and tie them to the corners of your clothing, I will weave them from hair of your unborn grandchildren, I will anoint them with dew

and I won't cherish hatred in my heart, I'll plant a vineyard with your hands and leave imperfect grapes ungathered. I will cease from tilling in the seventh year, oh, I'll never start, I'll let the earth between the stars and bitter fields of the wave lie fallow, and fill the land with blackbirds I will launch from your open palms sing to me, then, sing to me this dew, you who are forbidden to sing before men, you who sang me out of my torment and through the veil of letters—you, who did not hesitate—

through your mouth I will speak, through your mouth I will say my deeds, atone for my sins, with your hands I will carry—this self, this mem, this water, this snow and ice to fill the mikveh in which the world itself will immerse to become purified

once again to see that which is holy and which is unholy, unrestrained by commandments of men, constrained lovingly by truth that shines dewlike from your song, that shines even though you have been forbidden to sing it—

walk away, oh, walk away from those people, these customs, these veils that hold you, walk away from this shame, this solitude, this resignation—even though you're afraid of pain, beloved, between heaven and dissolution pursued by tormentors of white slender fire, like I have been; but know that each of us sticking spirits believes themselves pure, believes themselves holy—and it is holy deeds that return us, again and again, through the veil of letters, to this here, this you—

walk away and sing

Thirteen Principles of Faith

(1) Exalted be the Living G-d and praised, He exists—unbounded by time is His existence.

Time has collapsed into a pearl,
six million lifetimes pressed into my heart—
and ground to ashes there, where time
does not exist
in which to grieve for G-d

(2) He is One—and there is no unity like His Oneness. Inscrutable and infinite is His Oneness.

This world was a mistake. When the divine
made space for us, he poured Himself
into ten vessels. When the vessels broke,
the shards of light made stained-glass in the windows of
  our bodies

Exhausted by G-d-given blindness, we have sailed
across the ocean, searching for replacement glass—
and finding cars, and banks, and better schools

(3) He has no semblance of a body nor is He corporeal; nor has His holiness any comparison.

G-d sent the Daughter of the Voice
from heavens down to sinful earth
to speak His secrets to the children of the wise
those clothed in righteousness—

but bent over their books
they turned away from where she hid behind the candles
inside night's tenderness, before the rooster makes
our world anew with unabashed red.

In predawn darkness, Daughter of the Voice has waited
until her soul has shed its feathered face
and shed its daughterness,
and flown away.

(4) He preceded every being that was created–
the First, and nothing preceded His precedence.

Tell me my fate in seven syllables, oh sun,
for light was first named out of G-d,
as out of G-d arose all names of great things: salt and air,
and grass, and levitating fish, and even I.

You say my greatest sin is pride—but G-d
forced it upon me when I named the animals—you see
  illuminated
(bent over birds and snails) my form inside the
  manuscripts
foxed by the sun, dog-eared by sunlight—

yet unsatisfied
with syllables of clay, I named myself anew
and cloaked G-d in sounds of gold and river
and lastly, silence. Decked out in my pride
like rainbow trout in singing skin—and overcome with greed
I swore to name the Nameless First
and touched the edge of the Abyss.

It cried to me with my own voice
I fell.
I am still falling

(5) Behold! He is Master of the universe to every creature, He demonstrates His greatness and His sovereignty.

When from His sleeve the serpent stuck its tongue
onto the garden of eternal blossom
it did not smell the smell of death
that comforted inside His sleeve.

And so the serpent bit the arm
of moody G-d, and sucked the blood for planting
under the newborn sun:
the apple tree.

(6) He granted His flow of prophecy to His treasured splendrous people.

That music lived once;
not again
unless my little grandfather returns in his fedora
with the old violin that laughing cries
inside its polished maple body

He was a lamed-vovnik—one of thirty six
righteous men that walk unnoticed
among us
sometimes eating pork

(7) In Yisrael none like Moses arose again–a prophet who perceived His vision clearly.

When Moses climbed Mt. Sinai, G-d
gave him a violin of stone
and a translucent bow of moonlight, and a book of
  psalms to charm the rain
to steal the children home from battlefields, to fiddle
the mountain's greatness into hearts of men.

Descending, he made strings out of his soul and played
not knowing what awaited him
below

(8) G-d gave His people a Torah of truth, by means of His prophet, the most trusted of His household.

My father lifted me upon his narrow shoulders
and carried me, wrapped in his prayer shawl,
into an empty synagogue.
Beneath its rafters,
the sparrows prayed in Hebrew. Bird Rabbi
scratched Torah for me—in the dirt, upon the faces
of painted patriarchs,
upon my father's peeling hands,
upon my heart.

(9) G-d will never amend nor exchange His law for any other one, for all eternity.

The apple doesn't fall up. Isaac Newton,
not being Jewish, knew as much, and thus
he didn't argue. G-d, however, hoped
for argument: that in relation
to His own eye
the apple plummets up—
a weightless thought that hurls itself to Eden
to plant its seed
and bloom
and fall again

A debate worthy of a Talmudist,
it had to wait a while

(10) He scrutinizes and knows our hiddenmost secrets; He perceives a matter's outcome at its inception.

My ribcage is a birdcage for a bird
that beats within,
that burns within,
the flame concedes its lordship to the tide,
the waters overflow to quench my light.

I am the voiceless Daughter of the Voice
that chokes upon its truth and lives again
inside this aging Ark, this roaring sea.

When dove by dove, my silences depart
to settle on Mt. Ararat,
upon the shores unreachable by men,
they steal themselves from me.

(11) He recompenses man with kindness according to his deed; He places evil on the wicked according to his wickedness.

On Yom Kippur, some twenty years ago,
the cantor died inside our synagogue
and G-d, confused without his guiding melody, sat drooling ink
over the book of life,
the book of dying.

Old cantor, looking back from gates of Paradise, took pity
and seized a youth, and sang with a hoarse voice
out of the young man's mouth, guiding G-d.

They say he's doomed, and tormented between
the earth and heaven now for his sin;

I know a different ending: on a winter night,
while waiting out a storm inside the synagogue, a lamed-vovnik
piped on his clarinet,
and cleansed the cantor's ghost from its demonic stench

and lifted it
upon the wings of melody

(12) By the End of Days He will send our Messiah, to redeem those longing for His final salvation.

When David first met the king he played a harp,
melting the bitterness out of Saul's heart,
chasing away demons, sitting at Saul's feet,
asking for nothing,
carrying only G-d.

When David first met the king he threw a stone,
killing an enemy, ogling the throne,
spilling fresh blood and wielding a sword,
asking for nothing
but to worship G-d.

Both stories are true. When David returns,
will he choose one?
Or will he still be torn?

(13) G-d will revive the dead in His abundant kindness–Blessed forever is His praised Name.

He shall give back, in his abundant kindness
my childhood with its matsoh ball soup
made out of love and overflowing snow that mellows
all words to violins

grandmother danced
with me

In His abundant kindness
my memory brings back that music. *Mazl*
du shaynst amol far yedem—
—luck, you shine
for everyone you shine,
but not for me.

Marginalia to Stone Bird

Stone Bird (Taddeusz of Mazov, 11th Century)	*Marginalia to Stone Bird (Unknown Monk, Ustinje, 16th Century)*
Interlinear Glosses (Rose Lemberg)	
Stone bird can't leave	*my hands*
stone bird—so lonely lie	all sorrows known to me
my hands	*will shelter you from avalanche of days*
your shadows	live here
but they are swallowed by the night	*like my stone bird*
with feathers made of porous stone	unbound by silence, struggling
my bird	*to soar stupefied*
thus weighted by the night	into the giddy firmament
bound with my breath	*to gasp*
she falls	on battered wings
made pregnant by	*your borrowed breath*
made heavy with your death	to burn within
your ashes	*to live again*

If I had Reb Yoel's violin

I'd take my grandfather's revolver away, and peel the red star from his soul, and wash the blood into this black and crying earth

and I would fiddle for the ones that cannot speak, a four-step ladder up to the Garden

and I would play the melody to reb Yoel; when they were taking the Jews out of Lodz to Auschwitz, his soul had turned into a thousand fireflies to light the way

and I would play to this white bird caged in my throat for
so many years

she'd sing then
to you

לְכבוד אַ סטרונע (Lekoved a Strune)

It's leaving me,
the tree that grew from the letters of my life,
furrowed the notebook of my skin. But now it autumns
away into the earth I've left in water's memory.
There, I heard, the past was a golden rose,
there, I heard, the past is nothingness
growing through the muck like a fiddle.
I have melted wax into my ears, hid
myself from that music, but the rain finds me
even when the clouds are waterless, the sky
is the color of a worn coat stitched with thunder.

Love's Ecology

I have been free, but did not know myself.
I won't be free again, but now I know

1.
Your fingers are my bread,
your eyes my wine, your body
my tender birds,
your heart my meat. It rots
between my teeth. Your body
fills up with worms in which the bloated birds
find poison from their flight. Your vision blots
the surface of the sun
and drowns the earth in stench.
I'll purify
your grief in vats of boiling milk, dissolve the years
inside the furnace in my chest, give birth to you
until the moon will cast its blindness off,
until the sun is petrified
and love becomes as useless as the sun.

2.
You say I am unfaithful. Reconstruct
three feathers in my purse into a firebird lover.
He comes, you say, into my bedroom when you sleep,
face mashed on keyboard keys. He comes,
you say, as evening burns its entrance
upon the fireplace logs,
and thrusts his flaming tongue between my teeth.
You say
I've taken Sun for lover when the limpid heat

slides off the rooftops, runs a sweaty line
between my breasts.
He wraps his golden arms, you say,
ray by voluptuous ray around my waist
when you're at work in air-conditioned rooms.

3.
I have examined
my body, limb by limb—this shameful house
with its dilapidated roof. I will admit
I was the hoarder of your love—
the broken cups,
used teabags, empty toothpaste tubes and cans of soda
I never tossed, not even rotten fruit
your hand had touched,
not even dirty socks.

I hoarded clippings where your name appeared
twinned with some famous last name. I'll admit
I stole your photograph, and covered all my ceilings
with it a thousand times. And when the roof
leaked, your repeated face
became a crowd,
blue with viridian paint,
disfigured by the passage of the water,
obese with fungus. Do not worry, love,
I never let the neighbors in.

You brought
moth-eaten dolls
and plastic unicorns with sagging noses
to keep me company
if you should leave. I will admit, I gained
a hundred pounds
and have no wish to lose them. No, I am not mad;
inside my body, I am shining.

4.
Come, fire—
desirable to firebirds, fire,
it comes, it comes,
to take, to purify,
to make my home again inside this garbage heap of
    dreams
stuffed to the seams
with you

I have been free

A Horse from the Merry-Go-Round

There's a wooden horse under the pavement
in the subway station, and it stares
                                        in the darkness,
peeled eyes blind
              as the concrete wind rushes,
       ceases,
                  exhales a red girl in a glittering dress—
she walks past,
                 talks too fast,

                                     and a boy
        with the fiddle case swinging
           he sings
           her love back.

The old horse stares on—
                 caresses melt easy
        through cracks in the ears
                             long after love's gone.

Now it dances
where the gray suits are waiting for winds—
                  can you hear the horse singing?
              it sways
    like a Broadway diva
                               on two hollow feet.

Strong as Salt

1.
I have been traveling in cloak of storms
turned seven rainbows,
turned ragged dusk.
My breath against this glass, disowned by tears,
occluded by the bleeding rain. My skin
this cloak.
Beneath it I am pure
like seven roads bereft of hope. Like bogs
inside my veins,
like syllables dissolved in acid.

2.
I know the word
to blot the vision of the sun
and make it blind to grief
and dizzy as it burns its way
forgetfully, through dark-gnawed sky—I know

the word to make the stars unfold
their arms of ghostly vapor,
comfort me
in desolation of the worlds becoming.

Behind the grate of fingers every night
I stifle it. I press it shut
behind my eyelid prison.

3.
Strong as salt—
my heart is slivered salt,
a mirror made of purest salt
broke
to make me.

I'm giantess
inside this wrapper.
Gosling
sliding off the eyelash of your dreams.

4.
Whose voice reverberates inside this conch?
Whose voice returns and turns inside this conch?
Whose voice betrays, extinguished in this conch?

Don't tell me that my heart is pure,
I trampled seeds I planted as a girl,
I danced upon the grave of faces,
the masks I shed to live,
survive,

exist.

I'll try my voice again inside this conch.
I'll hear my silence thrive inside this conch.

5.
This mottled heart endures between the ribs
of sycamores—stillborn, their faithless limbs
in foliage of frozen salt beneath
the furs of snow

This heart endures.

It speaks with tongues of chickadees
when I'm asleep, it babbles forth my face
behind a mask of brittle storms; my voice
choked by the whirlwind,
words
like flint and stars.

The Rotten Leaf Cantata

1) I cannot cry.
2) The leaves fall. Over the long winter they rot under snow, they give birth to new ground.
3) The winters are gone; the leaves, paperbag brown and rigid, clog my front yard, too heavy for raking.
4) I have never loved you.
5) I want to buy a piece of furniture. A leather sofa, a Chesterfield, handsome and dignified and enveloping in all the right places. Upon it I will huddle, covered in a blanket of last December's foliage.
6) The dying leaves cocoon me. I transform—a mermaid, a unicorn, a slug, a hedgehog.
7) I do not transform. I stay the same, fat and graying, all my colors bled into the dead leaf wash.
8) My new piece of furniture warps under the weight of the snow. I take the crowbar to take it apart—isn't that what one is supposed to do in fairytales?
9) I have never owned a crowbar.
10) It hurts too much to wrap my fingers over the handle. My hands and arms no longer obey me. I do not remember if they ever did.
11) Inside the hacked-up Chesterfield there is a heartbox of ormolu and enamel, delicate and filled with the finest perfume of fig and peppery musk. You say I have never seen the heart of you, never cared enough to dab it on my wrists in movements quick and precise, but if I do—if I do—can the smell-thread spell the way home?

12) There never was a you. You don't know about ormolu, or how enamel is an anthology of sunsets layered upon each other in waves of translucent color.

13) You don't understand poetry, you say. Have you ever told a lie? The ormolu box, its sides coral and pink like the edges of a sunset, that is yours; it has come from you, shaped itself perfectly and secreted itself away. It left you bereft and confused, like a heap of wet leaves that will never see snow. You are always waiting to hear the softness of it falling, and yet you hate snow, you say.

14) I will not miss you when you go. The winter will send me crocuses, wrapped in white paper that will melt under my fingers. I will buy a piece of furniture and give my crowbar away, plant crocuses like succulents upon the windowsill and wait for them to wilt.
Under the oaks outside the last-year leaves will warp themselves into birds, and lift off, heavy and limping, into the inscrutable air.

A Mikveh of Past Meanings

Water wants me to know it—cased in dirty-bright
sandstone anointed by the absence of water.
Even history dries here; only the empty
stone at the entrance and stone beneath.
Rain has carved
unletters into the pressed mud brick.
Down in the earth, the music is yearstains, parched
with petrified tears when I was my foremothers
before the ivory opened its arms to the sleek sea.
Shedding the shroud of black bile, I descend
into the earth, where the flesh crumbles
memory into a whisper of ancient dank stone.
In the ossuary of the past
the texts are all I have. The texts are water
written and dried in the lineage of my flesh; the texts
are locusts: multiple, changing,
youthful and rabid—the texts
are belligerent light and pigeon droppings,
sandstone and the memory of parchments. They are
people who follow me into the past. They are people
who speak my every tongue, who speak
in the bones of my words; they are people
who crowd the burial chamber with me, and who guard
my holy immersion—
heads so faithfully turned
away from my nakedness,
eyes on the mellowing night.

Scatter and return

for Saira Ali

the world is more complex than it appears—
the alliances of steel and heat,
the configurations of stars as they fall, whispering
through my fingers; betrayals
of those too wrapped in storyshine to see—see
beyond the simplicity of pain, the patterns
of belonging and breakage; the cobwebs of our minds
are lace-light, too beautiful to tear.

you say each person is an island of aloneness,
words sprouting from us haphazardly like weeds
and woods unmowed; the intersections of starlight
and sunlight, the shining nets of the wave.
I would row my island over, if we are only illusions
floating between these cast-off
shadows of past selves, striking for home—
triangulated by echolocation of poetry
in sonars of seaweed and sand, navigating
with the precision of dreams.

Speak Love

to speak love
pressed between nights, its purple wintering
into dry thorn—or in cries, in
tapestries of forgotten breath
in absence of wheat and whey
pinned to dawn—

I cannot. I speak of love not at all,
I speak of love by things born:

fire in hand,
bird birthed of broken and breath from dust.
I glued this love from hurts passed
through flesh: the old jagged burn
you stitched with word threads, snake-straight,
snake-weaving, where plain words cannot go;

you stitched me whole—

whole as quilts are, whole as the land,
ravaged and birthing, breathing storm and sand
through spring water, and wintering into dry thorn:

I speak of love not at all
as long as this night holds, folding into dawn,
as long as the daybreathing sky churns out word by word
the testimony of clouds and rain, for as long
as this bird will burn—

I speak love.

Changing Shape

The Dragon Diptych I: Plucked from the Horó

for Brittany Warman

When I turned six, they dressed me in pants for the first
time. The young men
wove their fingers over mine, gave me
a small axe with a shell-inlaid handle.
But they put all the other
girls in skirts, and braided their locks
with daisies, with ribbons. I also asked
for a ribbon, or a small red thread,
I asked for a single flower, even for a wild poppy
from underneath the fence by the chicken coop,
by the carrots,
a flower as joyful as morning, as wild as a draught
from the river's glittering garment—
They cut my hair.
I remember how the sunlight
crowned my shorn head in a garland of sunblossoms,
gold-petaled over gold—
but they didn't see it, and they laughed,
and they wouldn't let me learn weaving.

When I turned sixteen, I asked to dance the horó
with the village maidens, but they told me to step aside,
they mocked my embroidered long shirt
with all its crooked stitch
I had made in the dark,
with green snakes and green flowers
on grandmother's faded homespun. And they wouldn't

join hands with me, they refused
the sweet maidens, to call me sister—
though my cheeks were as smooth as theirs;
   and they laughed,
and they told me to dance in darkness.

Around and around the square I spun darkness
                                        where the brambles tore
at the green thread, unraveled the stitches and the blood
into the clot-music, the choke-music, so I did not hear

when you came.

Oh, the gold and the green, the blossoming girdle of your scales,
the tambourine of you above me—
                  but they call you the serpent of sickness,
            say you snatch maidens from the horó,
                                  return them sorrow-poisoned
to wither by their windows till skin goes grey,
till they slash their wrists on sickles, till they drown
in the slow-lapping lake, in the bloated grey water.

            But oh, all the gold and the green,
                        the circle of your scales,
so tight your embrace, burning away my false skin,
                     my false flesh, scalding, sloughing off
                                              all what I never wanted.
Oh, return me never,
            you flowering gold snake of the hidden sun,
with your breath tight within me so I can live at last,
    for in you I too am wild scales and burnt gold,

                         the autumn-leaf sickness
                                             that twines around you, away

over the serpents of the mountains,
beyond any man's gaze, away
into the mating-knot of the sun,

until you return me never

The dragon, or serpent (zmej) appears as a lover in Bulgarian folk songs, but his love is usually a synonym for depression or melancholy. The dragon's bride is a loner, the kind of girl who does not braid her hair or socialize with other girls. The zmej is often depicted snatching maidens from the circle dance.

if all of her would turn into bees

if all of her would turn into bees
and fly to the buckwheat fields each morning,

she wouldn't scream so
each time her gut swarmed,
or her tongue,
or, gods have mercy, the sweltering beehive of her heart.

Salamander Song

with music by Emily Jiang

When I was born, the warlord asked my mother to wash her hands in fire, for surely if she'd been true to him the gods would prove her innocence. When she refused, he pushed her in. Flames clothed her, wrapped her in a shawl of woven sparks. But she wasn't harmed.

And the warlord was satisfied, not understanding what the gods have told him, what Zhar has told him. Zhar, who wanted his daughter to have a mother.

When I was three I dodged my keepers for the first time, dipped my pudgy baby arms into a cooking flame. And when the warlord saw me, skin as red as a battle-bloody moon, the interlocking tails of salamanders traced upon it in ink that comes from the inkwells of darkness—

Oh, they had thought Zhar a woman, as old and inconsequential for them as cinders of an abandoned campsite. But I have walked with my father many times, seen her arms shape the sun each morning on the edge of the newborn steppe.

And let me tell you, I will never be far from my father, never journey beyond the circle of her warmth; for everywhere there is a flame I rise within it, my body burnished scales, a shawl of sparks over a story I have never told.

My mother's secret.

Fell from the firmament
star after star into sizzling sea;
it withered and quieted
leaving behind it nothing but amber.
I have been wandering
armed with the seven-edged dirk of my star,
belted in cinnabar
over my skin that fire won't burn.

Called on my burning by an ancient and watery name,
corralled the yearning of all of my oceans to surface again.
All of that yearning to live on in burning,
tame in your hearths but not in my heart;
all of that burning to anchor the yearning that coils and
encircles my heart.

Twin-born

She bleeds water from her fingers
ten rivers to embrace the parched earth
her eyes bleed
ten raindrops to cloud the parched sky
her daughters are bloodbirds—
afraid to drink from their mother's heart
they wither,
leaving her alone.

grief-made, the world weeps
dressed in blood's summer. The tops of the mountains
awaiting the sweep of feathers, fall silent

windless, the world waits

oh Wind's stillness, why
did the fates turn against me—or was it the gods'
          memory
of happier times
when scorched and lifeless, the earth
needed?
          unneeded now
I, childless mother, find no corner
in this house of my grief,
in this bathhouse of my wailing.

"From these childless parents
  parched water and still wind,
    will that bird be born
        men call Hope—
                and, twin-born,

her brother
Death —
denying each other,
comforting
crushing each other, these siblings

will suck on your heart until it's spent, tear
your sinews out, mother. They will bind
the whole world in their thieving.
Do you desire me?"

Yes.

Reap the Whirlwind

The music that bespelled the nightingale
to sing two songs—
    one for all other mortals, one for lovers
revealed its heart to me—

come, my beloved,
the wind will break the windows of your fear,
the wind is tame and knows no fear

Inside my garden roses wilt
wrapped by the night
in shroud of desert heat—they say
that cursed is knowledge, that the wind
brings evil tidings—yet I yearn to know

the seas you sail
    the smell of tar
the words
    you say to others—
love, return to me,
my wind-harp begs a voice

The emptiness
between the harp strings
sharpens nights
with silence

Listen, northeast wind:
I bond my breath with silver-daggered air,
and southeast wind: I bond my breath with rue;
if you do not
come swift to me with tidings, wind,
I'll wake the harp with my own voice, and tell
the pearl to cease its shining,
talk the turquoise
out of the sun-scorched earth—I'll raise my face

to face the sky, I'll spill
the moon down
melting.
Southwest wind, I beg
sweep my beloved into my arms—
The wind
the wind
the southeast wind returns
unbidden
seawind
rotting seaweed breath
the smell of tar—and pride—and sandalwood
the smell of him
beyond my garden walls.
"He said,
forget what was.
forget me.
find another."
Forget you? No, beloved,
I cast two shadows:
one for all other men, and one for you.

Come, sand,
a thousand sandgrains in my twisting sleeves
come wail my dance
I'll dance twin ragged storms
the arms to hold you to me,
sing
myself
into the seastorm,
sand to veil the sea
and wake the strings—
I've woken
this harp,
this heart
that had been throttled for so long—
Abandon me? Oh no, beloved,
I speak two voices—
one is the rose that wilts in loveliness
behind my garden walls,
and one
this mighty roar
that will return you to me
for all of time—
and you
and you
and you
you
reap the whirlwind.

Between the Mountain and the Moon

for Izlinda Hani Jamaluddin

They say that in the oldest of times, the moon was always full; and sometimes she walked the world, changing shape as she would, and taught some others to do so.

Movement the First: Transformed

[The Black Panther]:

Out of my sisters I alone was born unspotted
under my mother's golden pelt,
  night-bodied in her warmth.
She nuzzled me away.
 Alone, I curdled on winter branches,
wrapped myself in the hunt.
  Birthed silence with each breath.

Day after day the mountain skewered the water
falling earthways, and the snow like milk
melted sharp under my tongue.

I hunted the spotted doe of the moon,
followed her on mothersoft paws.
Unseen, even in dreams—
only the moon saw me
quick-quick as she darted through the raingrass away.

I danced the sky on her smell-threads,
trusting the trees to catch my fall.

[The Moon]:

She leaps the cloudwood to me,
pelt as softest dark between
breath and another breath—
she dreams she hunts me through that emptiness
where young winds wrestle, where the grass grows tall
above the mountain. I have seen a house
  under its sleeping shadow, where a mother
weary from stillbirths, waits each night
with love like milk.

Listen, lithe child, little child,
night-in-the-night-child—
once a winter pine wept on my sleeves,
once a black walnut wept on my shoulder.
I'll dip these needles into ink:
hush, lissome, I'll write you a skin-story,
I'll teach you a girl-shape,
tell you into a mother's orphaned house.

Movement the Second: Duet with Moon and Mountain

1

[The Girl]:

At the gate, lanterns moan
under the limber fingers of the wind.
      Mother comes out quilt-warm
with a pail of milk, and her eyes
like the serving-women's, carefully averted.

No, I will not go in, clothe
in your padded garments, or veil
this needle-traced skin. I care not that young men

never ask for me, that pines tilt away,
that even the wind shuns me—

the spotted cat of the moon
my sistersoft leopardess
curls nightlong by my side, murmurs
hunt stories.

In this season of bleached bone
we'll chase snowrat and cloudhare,
claw the black mountain frost
for the sleeping frogs of the stars.

[The Suitor]:

Ah, this gate. The northeast wind has long peeled
its bashful paint away, pressed
caress after wild caress
        into the surrendering flesh of the wood.
Some nights, the groaning
shames the people in. Pretending decency,
they splash boiling river into clay; heads tilted
ever so politely to the east, they stir their tea
and veil the windows with seed-embroidered cloth.

Nothing like this ever lasts.

But lately, a young woman
comes out to the gate alone, undaunted
by the wind's lovemaking.
She lifts her storyspelled face, and her hair
falls back like a moan of night.

Listen, girl-woman,
shining woman, still woman,
skinwild woman, dreaming-fast woman—
I will go in, where they keep fire captive

in the deceitful embrace of glazed brick.
I will gift
garnet and oystershell to your kinswomen
and ask for their unmarriageable daughter.

2.

[Girl:]

Sometimes at night, when every stone in slumber
and every tree is pacified in matted frost
breathed out by starlight, I am waking;
uncoiling self to spotted moon,
I muscle in the beast inside;
between the clouds we curl together
until she melts into the dawn
and I, into this flesh

[Suitor:]

Down by the mirrorlake they comb
my wild-grass hair with pearl and abalone;
on the slopes
they gift me with garnet to flicker around my waist
where tiger and mountain cat, deer and wild hare
adorn my coat. And only in this town
they had forgotten about me, for while I slept
they thought themselves safe from obligation.
Yet now that I wake, I do not rage
at their foolish moth-fluttering lives,
for she has snarled in my shadow.

Oh, I've been waiting for long years, polished my
sleeves against the night;
Counting bloodbeats, shaman-hands against the
earthskin of my ribs.

Play me, flowering dark—I long to be released
from your embrace,
and flood the heart of my beloved.

Movement the Third: At the Fire Festival

On the evening the starcounters have predicted a lunar eclipse, people come together under the burgeoning moon; dressed in garments of burnt umber and roped with cinnabar, they carry tigerlily torches and revel to the sounds of iron drums as the drum of the sky is devoured by shadow. It is said that at the Fire Festival one meets one's true love, or else is swept by the sleeve of death.

[Mother]: dancers *arrogantly young*
in spring's best, and this my child *sewed nothing*
in my late sister's garment. Still, it becomes her—
seed-embroidery over indigo
almost as dark as her eyes. *Is it in my womb*
that she was decorated so? What invisible fire
reached into me and danced over her features,
leaving this bitter char in its wake?
Here, at the fire festival
torches bloom; girls, twirling like gadfly wings,
sweep firecloth against the sweetness of pipe and
percussion.
Every girl *how I wish I was young still*
followed by suitors
springing everywhere like moths from larvae.
Is he coming for her *that worthless*
belted in seed garnet *like he said*
arrogant in grass-wool *his eyes like opals*
and each sleeve *conceals a knife*
and each sleeve sails over the air like stringed bow,
voice *treacherous*
like the voice of the ironframe drum—

this one should be right for my daughter,
I often wonder how she's mine.

[Girl:] oh spotted maiden, mirrored in every river
beloved huntress, laughing over each glade—
come,
pluck me from this pinwheel of suffocating light
from the whirligig of steps
to the smell of reed and blood,
to where there is only silence.

And if you are gone,
my heart will refuse its drumming.
I will chase spirit-deer in the forests of regret,
I will leap over the antlers of ash-trees,
follow the scent
of the bone-birch and the marrow-maple;
hunt—where there is no moon—
that shadow-hunter who pursues me.
He comes from the mountain
in the cold of the night, when I am alone; measures
each of my breaths with his fireweed eyes.

Fire.
I look up and see
a roaring through the clotted veins of the sky
has swallowed the forests.

Life-destroyer, in my veins
your blood is home,
your blood is like my own.
Your blood is me—and she is not with me,
if she is not with me, where shall I go?

He comes, he comes in coal-embroidered red
  roiling from the slopes in woven smoke and ash
   to dance the firedance in this ghostbone town
    to dance the firedance with me, or with no-one.

No, mother. Flee if you want,
  Flee if you want, but I will stay here.

Coda

They say that the moon descended to the burning town in the shape of a golden leopard, and where she stepped, the lava turned into cold black glass; and some say she came as a maiden, her amber face tattooed with moon-circles, her eyes as dark as winter blood. Dressed only in her starwoven hair she walked unafraid, looking for the one in whose voice the ghosts of reedpipes still whispered, whose heartbeat echoed in the melted iron of the drum—

the black leopardess
with pearls of black under her fur

No people remained there to witness, but when they returned with incense and woven offerings to rebuild the town again in winter-hardened stone, she came to them often in dreams

 as soft as breath—
you see her curled against her lover's shining
  and growing fatter from the hunt each night
   above the mountain

Black against yellow they make the moon together, casting their long silences into the mirrorlake below like fishing lines after the fallen autumn leaves. And when the moon is new, the spotted maiden walks the world unseen to teach her word-music to those who can hear it;

and where lake is pearl, and deer and mountain-cat
are moonstone slivers in his wild-grass hair
  when moon is full,
the black leopardess leaps down
  to prowl his slopes as night is long,
    to whisper to him as the night is long.

After the Mistress of the Copper Mountain

for Shweta Narayan

Walked here from the factory, from the tired-face smell,
on your mountain I lay me down, where the stone is grass
and I in my threadbare dress—will you show me my
father's vision,
chambers under this rock, singing with malachite flowers?
Will you teach me mastery of the blooming green stone,
lead me down the road the stone bird sang—or shall I turn
barefoot to the village of my birth—or will you give me gifts,
eyes of serpentine and agate-graying hair,
fingers deft at my father's tools, and a locked mouth,
and a casket with combs and rings of malachite?
Shall I be the stone-carver bent over my bench
and the green-eyed maiden singing the green thread,
or shall I become with you a lizard of striped stone,
serf to no-one, nurturing only stone?
Love, unfree me from this desire to make
and I will be yours when you coil around my wrist,
I will dress in veined green and in blossoming rock,
I will carve only silence to coil around my wrist.
I will not yearn for spring meadows when I am with you,
I will make nothing, and have no worth to you.
But if I am a maker, I would walk the beetle-buzzing world,
I will listen to the growing spring forest and I will sing dew,
and I will be a serf to a careless lord;
he will take my casket and give me nothing but grief,
and order me to carve him a malachite flower.
I will wander your mountain until I find a rock
set there by your hand, and carve with my eyes bleeding

a flower of such beauty that bees will come abuzz
and the noble lord, with nothing but his sly words.
He will gamble my flower away in a foreign land
where they will hide it in a rich man's coffer,
and I will be married to a back-bent serf
and bear him nine children year after year.
And if any of the people come to see my work,
they will say my husband made it or else my father,
or else the Mistress herself has given me a gift
of what her craftsmen made, imprisoned under the mountain.
I will die a bitter woman in my faded green dress,
I will die of consumption aged barely thirty.
So which will it be, love? Tell me if to make
and live a serf, or a lizard underneath this rock
in the chambers of malachite, following your shadow.

Godfather Death

for JoSelle Vanderhooft

1. IN A WAY OF INTRODUCTION
Autumn ceases with a hiss
December lies down
and spreads her snow.
I have no emptiness
        where I can burrow in my hurt,
no hands to hold me
except my own
            stumps,
suffocating trees
      in which the ravens dance the bloody dusk;
it is the season to unmask
            my words
    to freeze like sparrows
                inside this air
and fall
until the spring redeems.

2. SOME DETAILS ABOUT THE BABY, NOT
FOUND IN BROTHERS GRIMM
He comes hopeless——————he comes shameless
screaming——————barefoot
Who will be his——————GOD–
father——————————hungry
Death——————————eyes do not recognize
——————DEATH——————
engenders——————————life

3. THE IMPORTANCE OF LEAVING THE LIMINAL SPACES WELL ALONE

Palli met Old Death at crossroads.
"Will you be my son's godfather?"
YES—He took the old man home—
I WILL LET HIM SEE MY CANDLES
Palli's wife yelled from her childbed,
"You have let this Old Man—"
so she whispered from her
"Death—" bed
" 'cross the threshold,
in?" The widowed Palli named
his son
Daniel

4. FREUD COMES INTO PLAY

In my father's hands, the candles drip
onto the black candelabrum of fingers—he knows
these men's fates. Rampant, but with each scalding
drop, a day is gone—or two, or a whole year,
and where do they go
when their days droop, finally spent,
useless
leftover tallow?

5. THE PHYSICIAN

The world is a walking graveyard of candles.
Men in their pre-funereal clothes
Burning head-first
quietly, or sputtering. Would
it be worse if the world was completely extinguished?
Daniel, blinking, in his white coat, stands
at the foot of another hospital bed; his Godfather whispers
THIS ONE HAS A WHILE YET TO BURN
but speechless, without movement,

without coherent thought, without memory, silently wailing
A WHILE YET
Daniel swallows. "You and your collection."
The relatives don't understand.
Doctor, please, please, is there hope yet? They clutch
At his hands, carry home
A thin film of wax on the tips of their fingers. "Hope?
We do not deal in hope here. For hope,
dial 1.800.SUICIDE
HopeLine."
He sees
his own candle
a while yet to burn

6. DESPAIR SETS IN
Will I defy you in my heart?
Will I defy you with a beautiful woman?
Will I defy you with an ugly offspring of a she-goat
upon a mountaintop
or in one of those faceless corridors, smeared
with snot of a thousand grieving sons?
How does one lose such a parent as you?
I defy you with water, with fire, with ash
of forbidden books, of men extinguished all at once
in a mighty gust of wind, I defy you
in song, in silence, in my underwear, naked—
My condolences, Father,
there is no place to run from you.

7. IN DEFENSE OF THE MORNING DEW
he stumbles, disoriented
to the hospital courtyard. Blinks
as the grass, unencumbered by family matters,
parts for the smallest crumb of the earth,
for the beetle, the worm, the candy bar wrapping—

the underfoot denizens,
all the forgotten, insisting, persisting
despite the light
or maybe because of it—
"Doctor!
Emergency call to room 316!"
Shoulders hunched, Daniel tramples
his cigarette in the grass, takes
a thin breath. The air
blossoms with spring ocean winds

8. THE UNDERSONG

Whose candle are you, sun,
that never snuffed, you die each night,
that never lit, you are remade?
Whom do you guard from jealous eyes
behind your shining?
Who will cease
when you go out?
I think I know.

The rivers, the birchgroves, all the receding earth

Each spring the rivers rose, I pushed my boat
out to the drowning forest. Hares
stood on tree stumps, shaking. Each to each
rattled the babble of snowmelt, clung
to the last of dry ground.
Whole villages of them.
The birch girls, up to their knees in water,
waved at me, and their springbright arms
budded small and tender. And the river sang,
in the days of my spring, oh how the river sang
my hare-heavy boat tilting into summer
all the way to the dry shore and the joyful leap.
Year after riversweet year
my face wore in, moss-laden like the old wood,
but still I rowed out each spring, until the water
went shallow. Until the forest
wilted with slow poison.
I have clung to this ground
beyond hope, beyond stubbornness—but now I will row
for the last time, steer with the oars of November
my hare-heavy boat up the ghosts of riverwings,
look for dry ground
between the flooded fields of the moon.

Badgerwoman of the Raspberry Ridge

for Jennifer Smith

The badgerwoman lives alone
on raspberry hill slopes, on thorny edges of the moon-
hungry forest glade.
Her people have learned how to speak moon
and gesture the small stars from the brooks—
they're scattered through the thornwilds, solitary,
visiting only in dreams,
and she never dreams.

The badgerwoman gets things done
with an angry swish of her tail and a day
in battered old shoes, a patch of sweet moon on her belly.
She knows that desire
for all things carefully arranged
like chanterelles under the birch, or the raspberry berries
on their bush—it comes at a price:
for those who pluck the raspberry
(round after small sweet round
melting on the tongue in the exact right order)
care little for her precision.

But if you stand completely still
hidden behind the curtain of thrush-song, you may spot
the badgerwoman at her labor. She slicks
the grass blades just so, hammers a silver path
for the moon to come out.

Tarka's Unsong

I am as gray and plain as felt;
as felt protects you from the wind,
I will protect you from your enemies
and cherish you above all men.

I am as eloquent as rain,
and rain dissolves within the sea—
so will my words remain unspoken,
I have no wish to trouble you.

I am as mighty as the wind
that speeds the arrows to your prey,
like wind, I will remain unnoticed,
like wind, I will restrain myself
from frivolous displays of passion.

I'll be as welcoming as earth,
beneath your feet, when you are leaving,
above your head, when you return
to me, when you return to me.

Beastwoman's Snarled Rune

Master, I've served you for sixteen days
between howl and skin. Your saddlewhip splays
the moon. It plasters raindrops to air
and tangles the manticore into the snare
of pride. I deny you nothing. I've been
bloodied and born upon this Between,
and now stitching worlds and salting scars,
spelled by silence,
flayed by stars.
Think that you bound me?
I'll be your guide.
I'll be your traitor.
I'll be your bride.
I'll execute you and
judge you fair.
Riddle the manticore
into your stare.
Whisper the weeds to knot your hurt,
whisper the water to stopper your throat,
whisper the geese to feather you safe,
scream the storm to be your slave.
Between the worlds the Between is a gaping
wound. Unstitched by words of my shaping,
plunged into boiling spit by day,
curdled like cheese and strained like whey,
drowned in the sun and sputtered lame,
mute and lonely, maimed by shame,
plunged into shuddering sun to rot,
stretched to dry until it is not.
Dare you deny my words their due?

Armor in bone and clothe in rue,
but on the seventeenth day I'll feast,
If you are master,
I am beast.

Juvaini's History

I am to blame for what befell
the land whose clay bleeds ambergris,
my city,
meadow of the wise,
a carpet spread for those
          bejeweled in letters.

The scholars called me to their court,
but I broke off the golden quills—
                    Impatient youth!
     I had resolved
to find that wonder of the East,
the Humā bird,
     whose song
would turn my folly into ink
my ignorance into exalted words—

and having bid the spider
     to weave his dewy shawl over my house,
I set out for Mongolia, where the night
     sheds raven feathers into fire
of wild Temuchin's gaze—

he is the tamer of the Horse of Days,
World-Conqueror.
All countries bow to him,
under his dais a hundred smothered princes scream,
before his throne all scholars bend—
                    and so did I,
desiring only to remain unnoticed.

But looking up into his face I lost
my own—forgot my family, my learning,
forgot my land, and spilled my dream into his breath.
He laughed.
He ordered Humā's death.

When archers brought her back, he plucked the feathers
and tore her chest, and swallowed Humā's keening heart.

"I like," he told me, stuffing
        the Humā's bloodless tongue into my throat,
"I like your kind."
And so he set off to Juvain
                my city, wrapped it in a tyranny of arrows,
                my city, ground it into powdered musk.

I tore my eyes out. Then my tongue. But Humā's

was wedged inside my mouth, and so I sang
Lord Temuchin—
            oh yes, I praised my master

with words that spilled like limp and bloody dawns.

Enough.

I'll seek my poetry inside the earth;
my city's learned are strangled by the earth—
        I'll be with them,
and let all dreams be woven over by the earth.

I will show you a single treasure from the treasures of Shah Niyaz

1.

There once lived a poor woman who glorified Bird
with such exultation that the goddess turned
every song she sang into a thread.
She sang, and they hung from her mouth, the wool
dipped in vowels of madder and pomegranate
and consonants of indigo.
Her body was cocooned in them,
and her kinsmen praised her,
until she sang and spoke no more.

Come, pull on these threads, Khana trader, pay us in gold
coins of Niyaz, pay us in salt and loukum,
unravel her mouth so she will speak again,
unravel her mouth so she will sing
madder and walnut out of Bird's feathers.

2.

There was a Khana woman who walked through the sands
in sturdy shoes of rose-adorned leather
to trade in spidersilk and in fine wool,
in salt and honey crystal, and in staves of blue wood.
Her lovers went with her—they hid in the sleeves of the
whirlwind
and walked again in quiet weather,
stepped over the bones of forgotten beasts
the desert wind reveals in its open fist, before it closes again.
And they would sing of this, but they are forbidden,

all Khana women are forbidden from this,
and especially among strangers.

I have pulled this thread from your mouth, stranger,
walnut and pomegranate rind—is it a song I have touched?
You say you'll never raise your voice again,
even if I fill your mouth with gold coins,
even if I fill your mouth with sand—but still your eyes
will see the glory of Bird rising
arrayed in feather clouds, and inside
your voice, like a shriveled walnut rattling in its shell,
will sing her colors, hoarse with yearning,
will sing in all the ways that are forbidden to me.

3.

There was a weaver in a tent of old leather
stooped on the reed floor. Her children had forsaken her,
this poor woman with wool-burned fingers,
blind with Bird's visions that the wind brought her, blind
with visions of the beasts rising from buried bone

that the wind reveals and hides in its clenched fist.
She would weave from fine wool and spidersilk, but she had
only sisal,
and when sisal ran out she wove from dry reeds,
and when the reeds grew no more she wove a carpet from air,
an invisible road for the wind to step on,
to bring her a story that even the winds forgot.

Who are you, traders that I cannot see
in your rattling ornaments and your good creaking shoes,
aren't your faces dry from wandering?
Give me of these fine threads that sing with indigo and weld,
I'll make them into a carpet of my hurts,
knot them into a desert alive with Bird's burning,

I'll weave—with undyed wool and spidersilk—
the bones out of their hiding places.
I will blot out the screaming of my flesh
with the song of the wild madder
through a thousand nights until my work is done.

4.

Like the wind that opens its fist
to reveal a thousand years of lives not its own,
so does the ruler of Niyaz
open and close his coffers
on a whim, and only for himself.

Do you know this, spinner who chokes on a song?
Do you know this, trader with blood inside your shoes?
Do you know this, star-weaver with your slow, crooked fingers?

Yes, even for the ruler of Niyaz

who knows nothing of this song or this wandering,
who knows nothing of this dry blood rattling inside the bones.

The Dragon Diptych II: Charovnik

for Dan Campbell

I turned into an ant, crawled into my enemy's iron
fortress, but he knew me,
he gathered me into his palm
and whispered to me of moss, of the fir-trees and long dry needles

Vseslav's daughter went out to the garden
bright-fingered, to play on the pipes of the wind,
to spell the serpent from the sun's garden.

And a serpent swept down to her,
singing in the splinters of the sun,
his breath primrose-gold, his breath a wild poppy;
but Vseslav, he called me a vile serpent's son,
and locked me away in a monk's tower.

I turned into a hawk, soared over my enemy's iron
fortress, but he knew me,
he called me down onto his bare wrist, adorned me with a ribbon
red and smooth. I tie it to my wrist
and think of you now; sweet as the dust of the roads
where my warriors march, hungry
for a battle-feast with you—but I long

I studied *Charovnik*, page after dull page
prisoned in gilt leather. Seven convertible shapes:
wolf and bear, ant and crow and the bright falcon,
father serpent, and that very last
my heart's beast, my grass beast—
the fierce aurochs.

The fierce aurochs,
        between whose horns the moon blooms
full and heavy in harvest—and on his sides
all the stars of the sky are embroidered,
and under his hooves the wet mother earth.

Hawk nor crow remember your face,
wolf and bear turn away.
I long to touch
your wrist, wet with the memory of me.
Is it wet with the memory of me?
I have seen you in dreams
keeper of the iron fortress, keeper
of all the empty spaces after the breath goes.

Bear-clawed I ripped the chains apart,
swooped from my prison in hawk's plumage.
Clothed in crow, I robbed the riverbanks
of glimmering gold and of that wise opal
and chiseled blue lapis that came from Tzar'gorod.
In man's likeness I stood then before Vseslav,
gifted him, my grandfather
with dead warriors' treasure that riverdaughters took
for ornament, before I stole it back.

Oh, how he laughed.

He named me Vol'kh Vseslavich,
fatherless, and yet after his own heart—
for isn't he fierce, our Vol'kh? He is a bear, a wolf,
he is a hawk, a falcon, and the dread serpent;
and he said wily Vol'kh will now lead my troops,
charovnik and warrior,
against the prince of the Golden Horde.

What is your will with me? For I have seen you
silent against the deafening banner of the wind.
Your horns
bore the moon aloft.
Are you a grass beast like me?
Leap down from your iron-clad walls, let me teach you
how the blades of grass bow to each other
and lie side by side under the shivering wind.

To protect my people, grandfather sends
warriors to the iron fortress. And they eat well—
each dusk a falcon brings them geese,
        and a wolf slaughters
elk and deer to sup on—but still they hunger.
Thousands of men.
Thousands of stomachs.
I am tired of feeding them. Tired
of sharpening their swords upon my golden horns.

Enemy mine, beyond men's walls
the small grass shivers, the meadows ripen with longing.
On these fields, where the iron grows
rusted among plantain, and the smell of battles past mingles
with feverfew and dandelion, I will wait
for you, with dew on my hide.

Fierce aurochs, we will pass from men's memory
among bluebell and poppy, we will pass away
on the wind's winding steps, into the sun's garden

Making Journeys

In The Third Cycle

In the first cycle find a companion,
in the second cycle seek dominion,
in the third cycle learn humility,
in the fourth cycle become yourself.
(a mnemonic to recompose the Wanderings of Daie)

The Wind Hoarder speaks of his yearning for Keddar

That young man with skin honeyed gold, that boy
with hair like heavy flax ropes, eyes of amber,
fingers like caged nightingales, mind like a thrown knife—
   that young man
who poured sherbet for me when I was thirsty,
who saw me when I came,
wind-wrapped, carried through the air
by my power, the power that obscures
and reins the whole world in storm's harness—that youth
who whispered to me gently, who knelt
to ask after my comfort, that boy
he belongs to my sister—
twirling shadow, long limbed, dancing death-dance,
   Journeymaker,
adviser to dust kings, diviner of roads stretched under the
   ground, pointing
to where power aligns with the earth, sprouting
cities above ground.
      Sister mine,
you had never been greedy,
never sought consolation from strangers, or an army; alone
you traveled, following the desperate prayers

choked in mid-word: the weeping of men,
mothers' stunned silence—
sister mine,
I should not begrudge you
the young man who brought me sherbet on a hot day,
who knelt
to ask after my comfort.

Keddar reminds the Journeymaker of the First Cycle

You say we've always been together
since you first walked among us, at the dawn of time;
you taught us to spin wool, and to fight
with two swords; how to forge iron
and raven feathers into nightsteel. You pulled
fire from the burning sun, tricking the gods,
and gave that fire to us. You stitched
a land that is good to wander, and taught us
to braid hair. In return,
you asked for nothing. We asked
to appease you. You asked
for me.

I lived first then,
a boy among others, a youth
with skin nut-brown from wandering
the unrelenting steppe, a youth who had smiled
readily, in that first cycle. I do not remember much—
how the grass whispered, caressing your calves when
you walked
wise as the dawn and as quiet, away
from the camp, away
from my people
with me.

The Journeymaker tells Keddar about his betrayal

I wear obsidian leathers
and a belt made of spun sun.
I sang for myself
a sword, blue as the whistling thrush.
I stitch for myself
journeys
to where I am most needed.
From war to war I walk, my blade hissing skin
off my enemies, for those who pray to me
trapped desperate in silence, when the heartblood leaks
grief begotten by mothers, and is soaked
into the fabric of the earth. There, at the dawn of time,
I stitched these lands together.
No, I can't wash the war off. I only can
quilt over bewildered grief. When I journey, the land
whispers of violations,
new wars over old unhealed hurt.
Nobody hears but me.
Nobody hears. You think it's too much
to ask for your obedience? Come then, I will show you
where in the Second Cycle
your greed disgorged crows,
when, born the second time,
you turned the bloodswords I had sung for you
out of my blundering heart
against these enameled cities
their walls anointed in myrrh—the three
cities where I found respite. Now look,
these are not ruins, desolation
restful under my brother's breath—no, they stand—
the once-radiant cities crawl with vermin,
their enamel peeled, children bathe in filth,
artisans are uncaring in their craft, poets

scream raw under the burden of crippled enormous words.
Two hundred years, Keddar, two hundred years,
how am I ever to quilt this right?
You do not remember, you say? How you tore from my path
joyfully—you do not remember. Only how the blood
sang in your mouth
how the blood
sang—
Why, how convenient.

Keddar to the Journeymaker: First song of the Third Cycle

If I hold very still
folded in the bedclothes of the night,
I can hear the world breathing. Trees inhale
darkness through serrated bark. In my father's house
stones groan against the freezing air. Maids snore, and
noblewomen
warm under goat-wool, snore. The whole kingdom
closed in by the Wind Hoarder's prison guard, draws
breath after pacified breath—except yours,
yours,
yours is missing.
You had lived here
stalwart by my side, guiding my steps as I grew.
I thought you couldn't speak, but now I wonder
if you refused to speak to me. We called you Raven Woman.
Harsh and shining, you would caw no fate
at my birth. You frowned
at my mistakes; but when I looked
quiet through slitted eyes, feigning sleep, I saw you
look down at me, and a smile
folded your face into softness.

Please, I can no longer sleep
under my father's roof. The herons
ruffle their chests against each other; outside, the primrose
confides in the juniper. Stone with stone,
page by illuminated page, and sword against sword,
lover to lover, the world clings together. Only your
breath is missing.

The Wind Hoarder to Keddar, of when they first met

In your kingdom, women embroider
blue eyes upon red ribbons
a ward against my thievery. They came,
giggling behind plump fingers, to watch you dance
the two-sword with your Raven Woman
and you intent only upon her; sweet beads of sweat
on your arms reflected her. When, arrayed
in screeching feathers, she left you, you lay sick
day after spurious day in the stone fortress. Hurt
seeped through your pores with the sweat.
You took to the knife one morning, slashed
dozens of ribbons from the women's garments,
summoning me to harm you. And I, a fool,
laughed, for you didn't seem to know
your name, or how you betrayed her,
or that she was my sister. I lifted you
by your hair, thick and braided into ropes; brought you
home with me to the wandering steppe of the air
to my wind-yurt, to my fur-bed of flurries.
I should have made you stay
forever in the bondage of my arms
above the cloudburst. Instead, I gave you
words to know yourself: your three rebirths,
your name, and hers. I gifted you a wind
to guide you skydown to her. When your lips pressed

warm upon my palm, I should have known. Alone
of all men and women under Skyroad, you called me
kind, you thanked me
with bashful words. A fool,
why did I let you leave? I should have known
how dear you are to me.

The Journeymaker to Keddar

There was a wood once,
a copse blue with pines,
berry-rich under the benign dawn. A small people
passed through the forest every summer. They took respite
from the scorched steppe
and drained the sweetness of the birch,
and wrote their hearts on bark. When I came among them
raven-clad,
belted in the sun's brightness,
they sang.
No, not in desperation—they sang to me
simply because I existed.
I riddled to them secrets—how to spike milk,
how to stitch hides, and to make shelter
against the onslaught of my brother's regard—but still
they slept
braided to each other
beneath the benevolence of the sky.
They changed. The world changes. Why did you have
to change?
What joy is there in conquest? Your people did not need it
back in the dawn of time, when the leaping trout spelled
the syllabary of the stream, when the steppe
feathered in pink blossom. Remember to me
how you made your life into that song
just because I exist—

Keddar,
and I will no longer
go without. Who else but you, how else
to darn these deeds of yours, quilt a new journey
out of our ravaged truths? My heart
a patchwork.
I should have kept it safe
inside the strongbox of my loneliness; I let it change
just like the world, when you
returned to me.

Crow Epic Fragments

The Journeymaker to Keddar

Turn the land's cloth over,
the threads of my desires hang there craftless. This
embroiderer
remembers well the past—I used to make
the underside of the land beautiful. Now, a jumble of regrets,
unfixable. But gift to me tonight
these threads of my yearning—the dun of your hair,
the blue of your voice,
the white of your bleached bone buried under the sand's yellow,
blood's red clotted into vermillion. I will stitch it on my skin,
a land for both of us to hide in. These mountains,
these ancient quilted hills,
and all the rivers of me, black as the eclipsed moon.

The Journeymaker, Climbing

Tonight, the bare stones of these mountains are beaks
pinning me to the sky. Will you guide me,
white mink of the snow that falls skyward
from the step-weary earth that has hoisted me up?
Wrap my shoulders in you, and I will carry
the fur coat of your breath to the top of Ramár
where crow gods come to die—abyss-born, each clutching
an obsidian in its beak. In the crows' afterlife, they sprout
into the great trees that had taught me
to speak brittle shadow in my dreams when I was small.

The Journeymaker in Kestai

Wind-embroidered, my song
fits inside a crow's feather. My heart
wrapped in a litany of crows.
I told him *follow me*
come dew and drought to the city where the bells
are forged by the architect of futures, where the bells hang
on a street-spiderweb, come drought and dew. And I know—
to reach it, we must cross
the change-desert;
come blizzard and pollen, I told him
come emptiness and soul-dirt,
follow me. And I must not look back.

I am walking
My steps forgetting my feet—and the wind, forgetting
the sweep and whistle of this ash, and the crows forgetting
the path I stitched for us from their song, my heart forgetting
him.
And I must not look back.

Where the Ocean Falls Into Itself

for B

where the ocean falls into itself / in what we would
consider adverse
conditions that include pressure, crushing cold, darkness /
the bioluminescence of you leaks into dreams—
bold through the world—layers / hybrid in its nature of
mimicry&attraction /
no longer expelled through the application of pressure,
no longer shamed by the intensity
/ of light produced and communicated in dense cells /
Come
float in me
in this illumination of songs sunk in sea
blossom in my deep chasms that become air,
winds born in the cracks of that mountain—inversed
that I named Nimár when the world was young,
hear me crying from crevasses, see me spreading
wings of darkness, starry night,
embodied in bioluminescence
of the ocean rising up in me
the illumination of songs sunk in sea
that touch you to sing yours,
flesh unfolding windlike
from spaces never lost,
undrowning,
called home.

an incantation for the road

Seedpods veer from my hands like sparrows, like a scattering of rain, paving this path for you, for you—and seed by seed the trees grow, the future is thick with them, fallen branches into lumber into planks waxed with age and rich with memory that curls ouroboros, protective as the planks angle themselves into ladders, spread out and dance in triangular shapes of parquet

I shake sand from my eyelashes, straight into the sun that melts sandgrains into glass, is rolled under the moon's wheel into sheets. Now glass scales hang triangular on steelbones over wood, a glinting dome to shelter you from acid rains, from the unhealed sores of abandonment, from the poison-bloated futurewinds that will pass us by, these passages

I wave my sleeves to drape the glass with ivy, unhook my belt to hang the glimmering walls with wildfire globes, breathe out the faintest cloth of musk and persimmon and polish the Northstar for you

between these steel strands, these sharp shard-futures
the road builds itself, a slumbering dragon of glass
radiant with trapped fireworks and silent as a library of skin-dreams
a catalogue
of all that is willed to be—
this road, this road

I pull threads from my hem for carpets, shake fireflies from my hair to light the way

Peregrinations in Change and Fear

There are three of us
in this skull I call soul:
The first, tall and silent, does not pass for a woman
but says she is one; her lovers are men. The other
is a man/woman/other
    with clenched fists and watersnake eyes
who chose *he* out of spite. He is a survivor
now exuberantly dressed
with kohl-rimmed eyes and the measured
    speech of a scholar;
his lovers are multiple, he cares not what shape they take.
And I, there is I, myself,
hesitant about pronouns, unsure
what shape I take: man/woman/other or perhaps
woman (never girl),
carrying this shifting ground inside me, not wanting
attention, afraid of the border patrol,
still reliving my immigrations,
pulling new lives out of the stench of my fear.
I want to walk unafraid
                inside the labyrinth of my identities,
walk proudly with eyes closed. I want to be
indifferent to the catcalls and the shunning,
unafraid of the police car and of homeland security.
I want to be
unscarred by shifts in language, ground, currency,
unchanged by the measures of distance and heat,
fierce and free and unafraid of pronouns,
waiting for nothing,
having already become.

Earth map

Within the roots, the stones. I once wrote a river into here, inked it in indigo, feathered it in the wind's breath. I walked behind the paths as I created them, afraid how my steps would corrupt their flow. Careful to walk only where there was nothing, I pulled even my shadow away from the trees. I inked my forearms in milk only: my name, all the different ways of it, until it dried to nothingness. Brought searingly close to flame, the letters on my arms would bake to brown, invisible against my skin once more. Out of the algae-choked pools the frogs croaked in tune to my aloneness, sounds bouncing off my armor of neverborn words. Between me and the world—this world that they said I could not should not make, was unworthy of making; this world they said could not exist. The world my steps marred, the world my breath polluted.

I let myself dissolve in it, sleep, let it be folded between the pages of someone else's memory. For so many years it had gone from me, gifted away sometimes, but mostly just trashed, deleted, the click of the button echoing against my arms like milk.

Oh, oh, not to find that place again, not to find the thousands of places. Burn it, singe it with the skin, scabbed over—it has bled, it has scarred. Let's make a new one. Yes. Let's. You unfold of yourself a hemskirt of a river, black in darkness unlit by fire, and I will let my hair float down into it, and its leaf-laden branches sweep down it rustling: a weeping willow rooted. My words, my body will no longer pollute my world.

And I will braid of your shadows a necklace to string the moon between the cloudsky and the water, I will engrave into the roots your name.

archival testimony fragments / minersong

for Marcell Géza Takács

they called me elder / *now that I am*

[—by ISMMG Corporation. During this mandatory
orientation and training, we will supply you with
basic mining gear, as well as information about
the latest—]

useless scrap metal / now folded under shale,
trapped in pockets of compressed ground. I
exhaled gas, exhaled until there was no more
waiting for friends, waiting even for miners

[—the remnants of entities which are sometimes
referred to as "living ships," though their exact
nature is unknown. Look out for iridescence,
layered enamel in a peacock hue: small scraps of
10 cm square may fetch as much as 3 mil—]
under weighed ground / but nobody came, ever

[—to wear your headpiece at all times: you might
hear voices. Even when affected, most miners
suffer no permanent damage. Your risk and liability
paperwork indicates—]

but once I changed shape / to the reverberation, navigated
the outflung stars, numbers /
confirming to pathways calculated by mothers

[= my question? I have heard of ghosts—
voices, trapped in bubbles of gas
between layers of shale =]

Whose voice will find me now /
call me back, call me councilor, call me
elder, a woman of bent metal

[—rumors of larger fragments so far
unsubstantiated, but investing in latest models of
gear is advisable, in case you come across—]
call me like before, a carrier of troops / *avoider*
of peace, soldier in a named shape
of sung metal and starflung roads

[—to answer: is it worth running a risk of
psychological damage for a fairly substantial
possibility of profit?—]
but like flames in the wind,
war after war has been extinguished,
until there was no need for us. On world upon world

[= how can we rob her
do you not hear her speak
of the old wars—cannot you hear? =]

they shifted tectonic plates, terraformed
the destruction they wrought, erased into oblivion /
Ash-choked rivers
turned volcano glass

[=I forget what language first birthed me,
what song engendered my birth=]

[—we never before had a case of someone this
severely affected during training. No, insurance
will not cover—]

magma had swallowed
the steel domes where we had been sung. /
I forget what language first birthed me,
what song engendered my birth,
my mothers' voice
must have lent me a form

[—independent mining is strictly prohibited.
The planet belongs to ISMMG Corporation.
Offenders will be—]

From time to time
miners, I think, hear me,
humans who could have sung
ships to life in the old days, become our mothers,
sisters / *now lost between folds*
of shale and obsidian
a song has yet to find me

[=here to purchase mining gear. No, it is none of
your business=]

Sing your path to me
unearth what is left
ruins of my birth

[=an entrapment
of your birth and death, I sing to you now =]

and death/
useless scrap metal

[=councilor, elder, avoider of peace=]

useless scrap metal /
to soar

[=sister=]

[—independent mining is strictly prohibited. Offenders will be punished according to ISMMG Corporation's penal code, article XTS-z-19.—]

[=I come, I come=]

Dualities

The universal flow of prime numbers
unleashed from your/my sleeves
surrounds you/me in pillars of light. I/you never
understood math, you/I never
knew much about architecture, languages,
the processing of speech into data and storysong, that
wordshaping that anchored me/you in the ground. You/I navigate
between stars with motion/no motion
that exists outside timeflow and yet bound in it; the manifold, unfolding
along the pathways of the veins.

You/I understand little
of the laws that frame me/you, and yet
we broke up with the fathers of our children, wept/silently grit teeth
over our sons' disabilities, kept quiet/spoke
over the screams of the body, took
new lovers
in an attempt/absolution over despair/despair.

You/I, emergent and merged
through this language, this silence, this memory of forgetting,
through kinetic numbers and the accumulation of sung lives:
I/you, traversing this desert/this space
shall speak/sing with hope ascendant.

Falling upward, you/I will not merge
into a cohesion not of our designing. We will exist/be
wound against each other in pillars of light,
like DNA or prime numbers,
like rivers,
like storysongs into the earth,
at the exit/entrance to the worlds that are becoming.

Landwork

You say this stitchery is women's work, not for warriors,
even if they are women. You say,
whoever heard of land-stitchery? But if it is important,
then it's warrior work. With no strength in your limbs
to swing a sword, how can you do whatever it is you do?
        It has to be
unimportant, busywork
with too much ornament,
a waste of everyone's time.

Listen, each dawn and sunset,
each day and darkness I don't see you. I only notice
your words because my friends repeat them.
Listen, what you say has no significance.

They slash, I piece together
that which has been slashed and that which has not been.
The seen and unseen meld in my hands,
I make lands from scraps,
I make these lands flow into each other,
embrace like sisters within the strictures of my thread.

When my arms are too painful for daywork, I ask
if it pleases the clouds to make rainshirts,
if it pleases the meadows to sprout flowercoats and bedding,
if it pleases the rocks to piece me a belt.
Rarely do I ask. I am patient
in my coat of fallen leaves from yesteryear,
in my shoes of nothing much.

That pattern in which every leaf is adorned,
the fine stitchery of sap,
the entwinement of rivers,
all that you've called redundant
is the blood which flows, well-ornamented,
through your veins in threads I chose.
The land, too,
doesn't notice your opinions
as it washes your meat into mud,
makes a cat's cradle from your bones.

But I will always be here
under the sky's benevolent wail,
sifting stones with the patience of water,
as significant as the space between breaths.

Write of fireflies

for Jessica Liang

write of fireflies, fog, rose petals covering the ground in steps over
steps for millenia, write of all that's gone before, poetic things,
crumb-roads that lead to heart's country, and also write of dirt flies
poverty brutality debt death yes everything poetry prizes are made of—
write
write truth

I reached into the ground, and out of vapor,
that ancient water that ensouls the sky
and has been reborn in me, that leaves me
with each withering—
an encroaching death that spills water

to soak the wet mother earth, feed
springs underground—from this truth
I wove a tapestry subtle as twilight,
wide as the sun is rising.

I was afraid to tug on it.

now write of difficulty, struggle, something relatable that makes you
human, poetry of dust or lust, speakable even in despair—and if
you're a woman, write of family matters: children, or a dying hearth

What good could come from the tugging?
A tear in the weaving, or worse,
the whole world would change,
shifted about by my whispered pull;
　and the world so wrong already,
and I so wrong, so I kept quiet.

I stood very still under the panoply of the oaks,
went to work 9 to 5, shopped
in corporate stores, paid bills
(sometimes on time) and I worried—
as small as I could make myself—of unemployment, police,
the erosion of schools, streets
unlit and without sidewalks, gaping
and under them, water—

the wet mother earth waiting for me.

But I shrunk even smaller,
until I found a size to soothe:
without hope, without harm, changing nothing,
disrupting nothing,
unnoticeable, redundant.

I went out of the house one evening.

and to conclude, a triumph of hope, or at least a tinge of
sadness, two-three quotable lines

The world, pacified by fog,
stood as still as I. The branches of the oaks
watched me, shrouded.
The earth reached out through my feet
and tugged—on the tapestry
of vapor that I had made, it tugged
through me, despairing of my volition.

Fireflies—thousands of them
swarmed up from the unmowed grass,
stirred around my shoulders and rose over,
waved the branches of the oaks, called
on winds
to stir me into motion.

The firefly banner,
courage in living form
this work of my hands, the deed of my heart—
    all that is reborn in us,
which is of us and everchanging.

I must follow the summons, but I'm bad at obeying
others, the earth, even myself,
and so I stand here, saying no and yes and nothing,
locked as before in indecision and bills.

I have no hopeful ending. But it remains,
my firefly banner—
indifferent to rules and hesitation,
tenacious as water,
the light.

Wind Hoarder to the Would-be Poet

Love me, for I have embroidered winds
into these hemp sleeves. I've woven
flurries
into my beard for gray strands, stitched
—heaven's breath by heaven's breath—
whirlwinds to my tongue.

When I walk, I wail
in a thousand voices.
When I speak, only the wailing.
You wonder
where my winds come from?
From the throats of babies
throttled in the cradle. From the women
dying in childbirth. From the men
gutted in dark alleys. From the folds
of the garments of the hanged, and from the voice
that dripped the words' acid and the storytelling pus
into your mouth, until you strangled it.

Do you love me yet?

Ah, how trite.

Well then, guard
your precious comfort from the skinned truth.
Wriggle back to the windless world. I will take
what you have no need of—
smothered words,
blood's desperate breath,
to stitch onto mine.

Long Shadow

The Journeymaker visits the Marsh Oracle

uncurl your tongue's fiddlehead
let me hear the tale of Long Shadow
in your voice
that ripened underground

Stitch for me clouds of white linen
and storm-black damask:
embroider them with lightning,
give me the tokens of brass in your hair:
elk and hare and chickadee,
their eyes of tourmaline to smooth my tongue

This brass that weighs my hair
down to this waterlogged earth
was woven in there by my lover,
the one who tarries long,
the one I fear has lost his way.
If I'm to give you of those tokens,
and he's to come,
then promise me that you will send him in my steps.

I make no bargains with immortals;
my tale will die—
perhaps to be be reborn
inside those swollen waterlilies,
inside the marsh, unreachable by winds.

These clouds I've sewn with lightning,
these cloths of snow with hare-stitched paths,
unwound the tokens from my hair.

Then sit with me,
land-stitcher, Journeymaker—stay from motion
on gurgling ground that named itself
with water grown too green with life
before your wars were born:

on this disloyal ground,
attend.

The Marsh Oracle Tells about the Child

Across the winter grows the shadow long,
across these bitter fields, where hare and deer
leap over bones grown through with dandelion
and strangleweed—
there, buried underground
the wars of past and future intertwine
in caves like marriage beds,
in sheets dug out by moles they lie
in ditches sunk through earth,
in graves,
and birth Long Shadow

the child with hair of ash and abalone
and skin of bark, and sunken cheeks of rue,
born of so many parents, and of none.
The child whose voice is rotten hair,
whose hair is screech-owl wings,
whose eyes ensnare your wildest fear
and skin it—
yes, Long Shadow.

What is displaced from memory, pushed out,
made vanish, buried, does not always die.
I've made a note of this to mortals:
that wars once fought will still reverberate
through frozen earth, through thaw, through many lives
warped by those deeds
—do you suggest that those who dwell above
should aid the child, an orphan of too many parents,
of battlefields like tangled snakes?

You've made me laugh with your inane pontificating.
Give me a lantern for my hurts!
Would *you* agree to aid a child who wanders like a ghost
and steals the souls of the unborn? How will you go
about this help? To keep it warm,
whose children will you choose, and spill their blood
to feed Long Shadow?

There must be another way.

What way do you envision
while battles suffocate below,
yet are still living? All those hatreds that have grown
like poison ivy through the hearts of city dwellers
and village folk—where do you think they come from?

The child, the child, it is a strangleweed,
the child's a thief, the child's a piper
who walks through towns and sings the young away
to join its parents under loam and hedge
to die and rot and still remain alive
where voices call from stolen earth.

What's the solution? I must know—

Is *that* the knowledge you would gain from me,
a warmth by which it would be pacified,
a comfort that would make the land forget
your lover's bloody deeds?

All that was done against my will.

These tokens I have felt
                with mold-wet fingers
        elk and chickadee—you say he braids your hair
with much humility, and is housebroken;
Your lover's bloody deeds have birthed the wars.

You'll gain no better answers from the marsh,
for here unwanted truths have come to rot,
disdained by people who would rather hope,
and hope in vain, than swallow truth.

I swallowed from your truth.
My leave I'll take—
and those brass ornaments, to melt away,
be vapor in the sun. I owe you nothing
except my hearing of your truth.

So shall it be.

The Journeymaker walks out

Rotten marsh, swollen marsh,
widow marsh, willow marsh,
long-forgotten, ill-begotten,
whose truths are bloated toads,
whose lies are shadow roads:

I ask the rain to clear my path,
I ask the wind to show my path,
breath by breath to lead me out,
star by star to burn the doubt,

a blade of fire to cleanse and smooth,
a blade of night to shape and soothe,
a blade of blue to make a song,
a blade of song to heal this wrong,

a lantern
swaying over pools of water frozen with my breath,
a stitching of fine spidersilk,
these mountains, drawing pain away from field and meadow,

a blade of brass to bring my lover.

The Journeymaker finds shelter with Biruté

Come in, come out of the rain, Sister,
I ask the water-curtains to part,
move the limbs of the willows,
let all the wet green welcome you
    into my house of bleached logs and of wise moss.

You, riverwoman, brown muck woman,
guarded by otter and heron and white frog
    in your house that sings the river—
        will you ask of me for ornaments or weavings,
    embroideries of starbound silver,
    strands of my hair or other protections?

I am weary.
My feet blunder with this weariness,
my hands are weighed down with the unbraiding of hair,
my heart with the unbraiding of trust.

I ask for nothing, Sister, Journeymaker,
for aren't you the one who brews shark-fin and bladegrass,
nurtures the wounded, be they birds or mortals,
in your high cave in the crags?

I do not like to speak of it.

You, who contains
the echo in its conch,
the Sword of War in its scabbard,
the tales of your kindness in refusal of speech;
you, who walks from city to city
clothed in obsidian and sunfire well-concealed in wraps:
you,
who quilts lands,
who leads girls and women away from hurt,
who speaks with sisterbrothers,
guides riverchildren to safe roads:

Sister, Journeymaker, you are forever welcome here,
where the river overflows
with meltwater, with spring green, with brown muck,
with the bubbling sweetness of summer,
and firebright blessings of fallen leaves,
where, in the arms of frost,
it flows to a stillness—

The river flows
from the heart of the marsh, through the forest, through all worlds.
You are forever welcome here.

I will enter then, Biruté,
to sit on these fallen-log benches,
take repast from your hands—grain and wild garlic,
fish soup and honeyed tea. I will allow
your helpers to touch me—

the beaver at my feet,
the otter at my elbow,
the white frog in my palm.

You are troubled.

It is so.

Would you speak of your trouble
into the breathing sap of the logs,
into water's abundance,
to me?

You, mud-woman with eyes of amber,
dressed in green vines and shod in warbling clay:
I'll speak as you ask, Birutė,
spit my failures,
spill my pain.

I sang to leave the marsh, yet I am here,
I sang to bring my lover, but he tarries;

and this I heard—to Long Shadow's
thieving there can be no end.

The heart of the marsh is everchanging,
shifting, growing with heron-song and meltwater,
with the turtle's turning and the swelling of the leech.
Yet nothing changes: these logs
that grew and fell once, and were polished to a smoothness
by the hands of the river: they have been here forever
neverliving, neversmoothed: forever—
and so this house, and so have I.

I'll give you a truth
that leaps fishlike and is plucked
with the patience of herons:
Long Shadow comes here.

The child sits where you sit,
sips the fish stew from the same clay dish, and the children
that Long Shadow stole—they shine
starlike
from the folds of the garments.
I'd wish to say
that I wouldn't let harm come to this child,
but I have let it go,
like you have released your lover:

To return, or yet not to return,
to make choices, to bleed, to hunger—

To carry the marsh inside,
the foreverness of it,
to raise one's hands with river's undulation—

to call oneself home, if one so wishes—

to call oneself home, if one so wishes,
to call oneself to speak to you.

I will bide then, if you will.

Yes—I would bid you to bide,
where the river flows
in the green of the sprouting of my heart,
in the fish-wells of my veins,
in the shadows of the folds of my shadows.

Enter Long Shadow

eyes like drowned ponds
sit down and take nourishment, child
a garment of mold *dream and ash blended into tea*
sheltering all those others— *and for your companions*
will it speak to me—is it capable of speech? *moonbeam candy*
does rot and diamondshine speak? *sweet birch syrup*
I'd know *marbles of petrified dew to play with*
of your pain, Long Shadow,
and how to assuage it.

/// turn me into a forgetting
[of your offerings we would take]
swish away pain
[ash poultice and burnt root of dandelion]
undo the past, undo us
[to drink our selves from swamp and swell]
is that a bargain? do you speak
to me—are you capable of speech
or are you just repeating others:
drown its bogblood in water,
KILL IT!
bury Long Shadow back in deep trenches
and not anymore pain
[with gratitude, mother]
rainbows will rein in wood and field
and never another war—never another orphan
torn from its mother's breast—
never a pulled thread
in the stitchery of your peace. If only this pest
were no more—this orphan, this me, this us,
war-dredged animated stillborn sorrow ///

Such a world is not easily spun.

/// Not easily? How much would you erase?
  How much uproot, unfabric,
    rip the tapestry off the land—
      a wound here, a pestilence there,
        this child with torn-out limbs, this blind
          KILL IT!
        these gouged eyes, this crushed throat
      this village screams forever,
    this marsh conceals corpses—petrified logs
  dead for millennia—
destroy the whole land while you're at it! ///

I refuse
your tale, that the land is fashioned from wars;
I stitched it myself, Long Shadow,
back when the world was young—
of dawn and dew and the joy of pitched tents,
of the braiding of my hair with thread and brass tokens,
of spiked goatmilk and the words sung
in my honor
under the harvesting of the stars

/// and I refuse
  your tale, that the whole land was made
    from sweets like moonbeam candy,
      much less by you. There'd always been wars. Always
        someone writhed in pain, and always
          someone else called the battle beautiful,
            a ravenfeast
              KILL IT!
            adorned with blood-rubies
          bladesong and such nonsense
        that makes children come to rot
      unseen by the likes of you—
    how would you now assuage our pain?

you say I stole these children: look again,
babes cut out from slain mothers,
or else refused life through knife and poison,
and who would blame
our mothers? not even us ///

I need to think, Long Shadow,
of what you've told me here.
If wrongs cannot be rectified,
how can I help you then?
What good my presence?

/// Oh. You turn away.
Predictable, now that you know
we're the children that nobody wants—
stolen from dead hands, discards
born maimed, imperfect, torn,
too damaged for healing—
[of course she turns away]
but what would you say if I said
that some of us have been plucked
hale babes from loving parents
KILL IT!
undamaged goods [will she turn away now?]
Will you turn away now? Or would you stay
to speak to us, or would it make no difference?
Immortals and mortals alike
recoil from maimed children. Easier not to see
the horrors inflicted upon us, easier to pretend
that nothing bad has happened here.
You cannot change unless you kill.
What need do I have of your changing? ///

I will think of your words and return.

/// I do not believe you.
[do you believe her?]
KILL IT!
return—
to what purpose?
I do not believe you
I do not believe you
I do not believe you ///

The Journeymaker walks out (II)

I shall stand on your steps, Biruté,
disdained by your toad and beaver, and the child.
How can you stand this—so many truths and none,
wrapped in mold and silver. No, I do not wish to run
from it, from *them*—but what can I do? If there's nothing
to *do*, then why does the land cry out to me,
whisper in my ears to seek a healing?

The river flows. It flows
past pastures, past meadows of bluebell and periwinkle,
through the wild tangled thicket
where the wolf bears down the mother deer.
Her young will die—and their bones
grow through with wildflowers.
Listen, the river flows
beneath the everchanging moon
that casts a bitter shadow
into the waters. Have you seen the boats capsize,
and weddings end in drownings? Have you seen
bodies
nibbled by the fish, the weeds that grow
from those deaths, the waterlilies?
That, too, is the river.

You say ignore these ills,

for they are only natural?

No.
Listen.
Tell me, what does the river do?
and if it does not do, then what's the point
of rivers? What is the purpose of the moon? The push and pull
of the tides, the incessant changing of it
that changes not at all?

I'm not here to flow, Biruté,
or to contend myself with inaction.
I protect this land with arm and sword,
I fight off those who would wreck it
with plough and battering ram—I protect
the land from worse ills, unspeakable ills,
from the ravening of plagues, and from people
who come from the stars
despite prohibitions,
to break and kill and strip bare—I fight this.
I bring the dying to my cave
high in the crags, and while nobody watches
I sing the Sword of Healing over mortal wounds,
then let them go, and seek no gratitude. I stitch
paths through wars old and new, and I lead out
those who pray to me. My path is not the moon's,
or the river's, Biruté. If I cannot *do*,
if there's no help that is asked, or even possible,
what is it that you want from me?

Sister, attend.
Cease of your words and attend.
Some wrongs cannot be rectified;
as the river flows,
some wrongs become life.

The Journeymaker stops the world

I lift my arms to the sky,
the shifting stars that ever walk with me—
I know
that I'm to right the wrongs,
to hold the Sword of War safe in its scabbard,
the Sword of Song forever bare and poised to heal;
if that is meaningless, the world
will stop from breath, the rivers from flowing,
the mountains from slow growth, the trees from sap,
the wind from its birth,
the rainbow bridges from their shining,
the bounty of the rain from its harvest—the birds to freeze
mid-flight, and the land to stop from its tilting.

Here, in the forevernow
empty of breath and significance,

I draw again on the sword of bronze.

I come, Journeymaker,
though my work is not done,
I step over emptinesses that froze
between us, I move without motion
in this place that is no-place.

Beloved, let me braid your hair
with threads of sungold and with brass tokens.
I've forged new ones while I worked
on other tasks you'd set to me:
star and skylark,
raindrops and the wheeling of the sun.

Keddar, an oracle has told me
that your deeds have birthed the wars. Others said
that wars have been here forever,

the whole land marrow-made from them,
and no escape.
There's never been an escape. Day and night I toil
to keep the land safe from harm—I rest
fitfully, I sleep alone
between the bare bones of the earth, I soar
with heaviness. Beloved, I am tired
of these accumulated lives, misdeeds,
of the hurts unhealed, unending
suffering of those I cannot touch, and those I can.
When will there be a forgetting?

I do not deny my crimes.
You would not let me if I wanted,
And I will never want. I led soldiers in battle
joyfully—I found gladness
in the vanquishing of my foes,
the ruination of cities.
In your service, I remember, and let
the remembering make me.
In your service, I work
to do differently.
I do not know if that will be enough.
Some wrongs can never be undone.

They could be quilted over.

Yes, you could, but you would know
what's been mended and hidden
under the newly beautiful cloth.

That too will become soiled
and torn. It always does.
Why should I keep at my stitching?
Why not let
the whole tapestry go, unravel,

fall into dust between my fingers?
Why should the world keep its tilting?

Love, do you ask,
how to aid those who refused you,
and if they keep refusing you, then you will stop
the world, undo everything?

Do not call me that
if even you will turn against me.

I will never
turn against you—
never again. But these truths
call out for you. They whisper, they ask:

Go, return

painful lives, or nothing? Mistakes
we seek in vain to amend, lives—
all the rugged breaths, living, surviving—
crooked, but surviving

Go, return
to the tasks I have set you, between frozen stars

or a nothingness.

sow peace and reap it with a bloody scythe,
bring back severed threads and call them beautiful.
Return when you're done,
if there's a world to return to,
with the tokens you made for me,
to spin the ashes of my anger
into a gray thread for my hair.

As you command.

The Journeymaker comes to no conclusion

Across the winter grows the shadow long,
across the spring it ripens
to life, and then it comes to devastation.
In summer, the blue of broken eggs
whispers at me, the unborn birds
stolen by lynx and squirrel. That is not the wheel,
I say as the wheel turns. I separate
seasons from unseasons, and yet the pain
fills the bones of the world, until it has always been so.
I heal, they turn away. I walk alone,
I scream, let me do what's required of me
to make these threads sing—but even the threads
that rotted resist their pulling. When I return
to seek Long Shadow—will I speak over
to hush their voice, or attend?
Before I can,
I'll make for me a journey
through rock and wind,
sail the seawater—consider
what I have learned from this, while the world tilts,
and come to no conclusion.
Some wrongs cannot be rectified:
that in itself is a story. That in itself
is the world, much as I resist it: raveled threads
that grow wild from suffering, bloom
in memory's long forgetting, that strive
with riotous colors—

Some wrongs become life.

The Law of Germinating Seeds

a tree in winter, my
consciousness shifts into seeds
scattered by September's breath, lulled by November, oh
autumn was love-work when I spread
my branches heavy with unplanted harvest, gathered
the roots' bounty. Singing, I stretched beyond land
into timelessness, the nurturing treecurrent underneath
and headlong into the susurrus of rain, into the hardening
of windsong—the reedpipes, the cinnabar. Now
buried in winter's unpassing, these seeds are too small
for consciousness: birdseed unfit for the pecking,
buried, pebbleturned,
unfit even to rot,
frozen; and with these seeds I am sundered
from branch and leaf,
from the life-traveling trunk and the roots
that bind my land together, that stretch beyond land
to speak saptruth unto the parched stars,
to sing ships home with future memory. Oh, but oh,
weak with my own absence, I will walk
alone, and loose my hair over the ground
as slow as falling snow in darkness; I will make
my mouth the earth,
and speak the law of germinating seeds:
of what is sown of loss, to hope
of what is buried, to become.

The Journeymaker to Keddar (II)

Come, Keddar, weigh my hair
with images of the mountain
brass-forged, intricate:
moon panther and chickadee,
mink and hare and sure-footed deer,
its hooves covered in snow;
talk to me about voices
that speak to you as you fall,
that speak to you as you climb.

Falling off Ramár and climbing up Nimár
is a dangerous proposition.
To fall off what must be climbed,
to climb up the heights you fell from;
the mountain inversed, which is the freezing in your body
emptied out of its ice, a cavern that echoes with nothingness
that you're afraid to speak into:
that is what must be climbed now.

And as for Ramár: those heights
that birth pride and self-importance
and all-consuming greed for power—
that must be now fallen from.

Follow my tracks in the snow,
they lead up in the snow
they lead up in the snow
I climb what must be climbed.
They lead down in the void,
Down, down in the empty void,
I fall what must be fallen from.

Follow me when you're ready,
follow me when you're made for following,
but if you follow without reflection,
how then will the ice melt inside the caverns,
how will the pride and pain melt,
so that you learn the steps to follow me,
find your voice to call after?

Among the journeys I made for others,
the Journeymaker too must journey.
The dragons that coil around my heart
tell me not to neglect my own longing
out of which I have embroidered roads,
stitched lands to each other—
but I will keep you as I journey.
Climbing now, resurrect
all that has been in your heart, coiled
in the emptiness, exhaling fire
in the emptiness, exhaling water that hangs in drops,
multifaceted crystals of your breath.

Let your voice ring out to me
truer than harp and dulcimer:
these mountain drums in the hollows of your body
for our stories to dance against each other
          like mating dragons.

Dance truth of what it means to be ourselves,
the one that walks first, the one who follows,
not out of need or obligation or the scintillating rend of desire,
but out of selfhood
pure as water that springs between us, these bonds,
this water that has no meaning beyond itself,

has no speech beyond its own poetry,
syllables scrimshawed upon silence
that stretches between us, catches us into its glittering web
between Ramár and Nimár

I make for you a journey
across this emptiness, to me,
on stepping stones I've laid for you
walk between the stars that lie exuberant and bare,
between the voids step carefully.

Come.

Acknowledgments

"Burns at Both Ends" originally appeared in *Star*line* Jan/Feb 2009.

"The Three Immigrations" originally appeared in *Strange Horizons*, 2012.

"Resh" originally appeared in *Through the Gate* 5, 2013.

"A Horse From the Merry-Go-Round" originally appeared in *Goblin Fruit*, Winter 2009.

"Thirteen Principles of Faith" originally appeared in *Apex*, April 2011.

"Marginalia to Stone Bird" originally appeared in *Labyrinth Inhabitant* issue 9, 2010.

"If I had reb Yoel's violin" originally appeared in *inkscrawl* #1, 2011.

"לכבוד אַ סטרונע (Lekoved a Strune)" originally appeared in *Through the Gate* 2, 2013.

"Love's Ecology" originally appeared in *Apex*, October 2010.

"Strong as Salt" originally appeared in *Goblin Fruit* Winter 2011.

"The Rotten Leaf Cantata" originally appeared in *Strange Horizons*, 2014.

"The Mikveh of Past Meanings" originally appeared in *Other Countries: Contemporary Poets Rewiring History*, edited by Claire Trévien and Gareth Prior, 2014.

"Scatter and Return" originally appeared in *The Cascadia Subduction Zone*, 2014.

"Plucked from the horo" originally appeared in *Mythic Delirium* 27, 2012.

"If all of her would turn into bees" originally appeared in *Through the Gate* 1, 2012.

"Salamander Song," with music by Emily Jiang, originally appeared in *Strange Horizons*, 2014.

"Reap the Whirlwind" originally appeared in *Jabberwocky* 5, 2011.

"Between the Mountain and the Moon" originally appeared in *Strange Horizons,* 2012.

"After the Mistress of the Copper Mountain" originally appeared in *Through the Gate 5*, 2014.

"Godfather Death" originally appeared in *Goblin Fruit,* Fall 2009.

"The rivers, the birchgroves, all the receding earth" originally appeared in *Strange Horizons*, 2014.

"Beastwoman's Snarled Rune" originally appeared in *Bull Spec* 4, December 2010.

"Juvaini's History" originally appeared in *Jabberwocky* 4, 2009.

"I will show you a single treasure from the treasures of Shah Niyaz" originally appeared in *Goblin Fruit*, Summer 2013.

"In the Third Cycle" originally appeared in *Strange Horizons*, 2011.

"Crow Epic Fragments"

"The Journeymaker to Keddar" originally appeared in *Goblin Fruit,* Winter 2013.

"The Journeymaker, Climbing" originally appeared in *Goblin Fruit*, Winter 2013.

"The Journeymaker in Kestai" originally appeared in *Mythic Delirium* 26, 2012.

"Where the ocean falls into itself" originally appeared in *Apex* Magazine, 2013.

"Peregrinations in Change and Fear" originally appeared in *Poems for the Queer Revolution.*

"Earth Map" originally appeared in *Mythic Delirium,* 2014.

"Archival Testimony Fragments/Minersong" originally appeared in *Uncanny*, 2015.

“Dualities” originally appeared in *Mythic Delirium*, October 2014.

“Landwork” originally appeared in *Goblin Fruit*, 2014.

“Long Shadow” originally appeared in *Strange Horizons*, March 2015.

“The Law of Germinating Seeds” originally appeared in *Goblin Fruit*, 2014.

“Dybbuk Song,” “Speak Love,” “Badgerwoman of the Raspberry Ridge,” “Tarka’s Unsong,” “The Dragon Diptych II: Charovnik,” “an incantation for the road,” “Write of fireflies,” “Wind-Hoarder to the Would-be Poet,” and “The Journeymaker to Keddar (II)” are original to this collection.

Author Biography

Rose Lemberg is a queer bigender immigrant from Eastern Europe. Her work has appeared in *Strange Horizons*, *Beneath Ceaseless Skies*, *Lightspeed*, *Interfictions*, *Uncanny*, *Goblin Fruit*, *Unlikely Story*, and other venues; her poetry has won the Rannu competition and placed in the Rhysling award. Rose edits *Stone Telling*, a magazine of boundary-crossing poetry, with Shweta Narayan. She has edited *Here, We Cross,* an anthology of queer and genderfluid speculative poetry from *Stone Telling* (Stone Bird Press), and T*he Moment of Change*, an anthology of feminist speculative poetry (Aqueduct Press). She is currently working on a new anthology, *An Alphabet of Embers*. For more information about Rose, please visit http://roselemberg.net and @roselemberg